D0761739

Generously Donated By

Richard A. Freedman
Trust

Albuquerque / Bernalillo County
Library

the pop classics series

#1 *It Doesn't Suck.*

Showgirls

#2 *Raise Some Shell.*

Teenage Mutant Ninja Turtles

#3 *Wrapped in Plastic.*

Twin Peaks

#4 *Elvis Is King.*

Costello's My Aim Is True

39075047695645

elvis is king.

costello's my aim is true

richard crouse

ecwpress

Copyright © Richard Crouse, 2015

Published by ECW Press
665 Gerrard Street East
Toronto, Ontario M4M 1Y2
416-694-3348 / info@ecwpress.com

All rights reserved. No part of this publication may be reproduced, stored in a retrieval system, or transmitted in any form by any process — electronic, mechanical, photocopying, recording, or otherwise — without the prior written permission of the copyright owners and ECW Press. The scanning, uploading, and distribution of this book via the Internet or via any other means without the permission of the publisher is illegal and punishable by law. Please purchase only authorized electronic editions, and do not participate in or encourage electronic piracy of copyrighted materials. Your support of the author's rights is appreciated.

Editors for the press:
Jennifer Knoch and Crissy Calhoun
Series proofreader: Avril McMeekin
Cover and text design: David Gee

Library and Archives Canada Cataloguing in Publication

Crouse, Richard, 1963–, author
Elvis is king : Costello's My aim is true / Richard Crouse.

Issued in print and electronic formats.
ISBN 978-1-77041-188-3 (pbk)
Also issued as: 978-1-77090-659-4 (pdf)
978-1-77090-660-0 (epub)

1. Costello, Elvis—Criticism and interpretation.
2. Rock music—History and criticism. I. Title.

ML420.C841C95 2015 782.42166092
C2014-902537-8 C2014-902538-6

Printing: Norecob 5 4 3 2 1
PRINTED AND BOUND IN CANADA

The publication of *Elvis Is King* has been generously supported by the Canada Council for the Arts which last year invested $157 million to bring the arts to Canadians throughout the country, and by the Ontario Arts Council (OAC), an agency of the Government of Ontario, which last year funded 1,793 individual artists and 1,076 organizations in 232 communities across Ontario, for a total of $52.1 million. We also acknowledge the financial support of the Government of Canada through the Canada Book Fund for our publishing activities, and the contribution of the Government of Ontario through the Ontario Book Publishing Tax Credit and the Ontario Media Development Corporation.

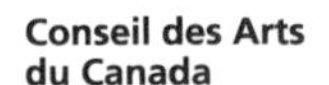

To Andrea,
"still, you are the only one."

Contents

Introduction

Liverpool, Nova Scotia, is the hub of the Lighthouse Route's scenic drive along the province's South Shore. Blessed by Mother Nature, it's picturesque, bookended by beautiful beaches, parks, and forests. As the home of the third oldest lighthouse in the province, it's also rich in history but not exactly the center of the pop culture universe.

Even less so in the 1970s when, as a music and movie obsessed kid, I went to Emaneau's Pharmacy every week to pick up magazines like *Hit Parader* and *Rona Barrett's Hollywood*. Perhaps because I grew up in a renovated vaudeville theater (it's true!) I was deeply interested in a world that seemed very far away, and those weekly and monthly magazines were my only connection to music and movie stars.

Liverpool wasn't on the flight plan for the people I saw in those pages.

Sure, there were rumors that James Taylor and Carly Simon had a beach house nearby, but nobody ever saw them at Wong's Restaurant, the only eatery in town. And Walter

Pidgeon was thought to have come to visit an old friend, but the *Mrs. Miniver* star, who was born in 1897, wasn't quite cool enough to be on my list of must-meets or even must-get-a-glimpse-ofs.

Those magazines were my only source. The local movie theater — a gigantic renoed opera house — was months behind in getting the new releases, and local department stores like Steadman's and Metropolitan (known locally as the Metoplitan because of the blown-out "r" and "o" bulbs on the sign that was never repaired) didn't carry the LPs I was reading about. On paper, I read about The Ramones, Television, the Sex Pistols, learning everything there was to know about the brash new music coming out of New York and London — Johnny Rotten said "fuck" on national television! — before I had ever heard a note of their music. Somehow, though, I knew I would love it.

One singer grabbed my attention above all others. Elvis Costello.

Maybe it was the glasses. I wore specs at a time when no rock star had eyewear unless they were impossibly cool Ray-Bans to shade delicate, hungover eyes from the public glare.

Maybe it was the name. To me, Elvis Presley was the irrelevant Vegas act my Aunt Jackie listened to, but I liked the a) ambition or b) possible foolhardiness of taking the name of the King of Rock and Roll.

Most of all, I loved his story.

Like me, he was raised in Liverpool — OK, it was Liverpool, England, but we both grew up on the banks of a river called Mersey, just in different countries.

I dug that he recorded his first album in just 24 hours while playing hooky from his day job as an IBM 360 computer operator in a "vanity factory." How cool was it that he got arrested after strapping an amplifier to his back and busking for CBS executives on a busy London street?

In 1978, I asked my brother, Gary, who had wised up and moved out of Liverpool, to hunt down an LP called *My Aim Is True* by this guy named Elvis Costello. Gary knew his way around a record store and on his next visit home brought a stack of records, the likes of which would never find their way to the racks at Steadman's. *Leave Home* by The Ramones. *Low* by David Bowie. *Marquee Moon* by Television and *Little Queen* by Heart. He missed the mark on that last one, but on top of the pile was the record I had read so much about.

Framed by a checkerboard pattern with inlaid lettering that reads *Elvis Is King* was a garish, yellow-tinted photo of a knock-kneed, bespectacled rock star in waiting. His dark rims — Buddy Holly was the last of the greats to wear horn-rims — framed intense-looking eyes.

Discarding the cellophane, I threw the record on my cheap Lenco turntable. Here's where the story gets hazy. I remember the opening line of "Welcome to the Working Week," and although I didn't have a clue what "rhythmically admired" meant, I understood I would never have to listen to the corporate rock of the Little River Band or Pablo Cruise ever again.

Finally someone was making music that spoke to me. Even if I didn't get the lyrics — we didn't hear a lot about the former leader of the British Union of Fascists Oswald Mosley in my

Liverpool — I understood the passion. I got the anger. It also had a good beat and you could dance to it.

I listened to side one through to the needle hitting the smooth space before the paper label. "Welcome to the Working Week," "Miracle Man," "No Dancing," "Blame It on Cain," "Alison," "Sneaky Feelings," and "Watching the Detectives." Nineteen minutes and 20 seconds of something I'd never heard before.

Flip. Side two. "(The Angels Wanna Wear My) Red Shoes," "Less Than Zero," "Mystery Dance," "Pay It Back," "I'm Not Angry," and "Waiting for the End of the World." Sixteen minutes and 33 seconds.

Just under 40 minutes of pop-punk songs that changed everything for me. I flipped that record over, and over, and over until I knew the words to all the songs. From that moment on, I would never again listen to music that didn't speak directly to me. It turned me into an exacting — and probably sometimes insufferable — music fan no longer sated by the sugary sounds that spilled out of my radio.

To me, this was art. The slick sounds of REO Speedwagon, Air Supply, et al. may have been more ear-friendly, but this was visceral. I heard the snarl in Elvis's voice, the cynicism dripping off every line, and, for me, that was the noise that art made. It was liberation from my small town.

Lines like about women filing their nails and dragging the lake had no connection to my life, but the delivery system — Elvis's raw energy and anger — spoke to me in a way nothing had before. The music came lunging at me like a drunk with a broken bottle. I have never forgotten it.

He sang like he meant it. He sang like he was bored, mad, and bored of being mad.

He sang like I felt. He sang to me.

When I first started listening to *My Aim Is True* and then, years later, began writing this book, I regarded Elvis Costello as a fully formed entity, a mature artist who had burst on to the scene, rarin' to rock. During the writing of the book, however, I spent hours listening to the album in a way I never had before.

I played each song on permanent repeat until I had an Elvis epiphany. Listening to his youthful, vital wail, I realized he wasn't formed at the time, but a burgeoning artist, bursting at the seams. The cumulative effect of years of rejection and indifference, coupled with the excitement he must have felt at finally recording an album with real musicians, surges off the record, jumping out of the grooves. He was caught on the threshold between Declan MacManus and Elvis Costello, between being a family man in a dead end job and the vitriolic singer-songwriter pushing against the conventions of the music industry.

The British music scene was in a similar period of flux, the aging rockers growing complacent, the young punks hammering at the door. In a year populated with classic records, his idiosyncratic collection of pop songs stood out with its sometimes-inscrutable lyrics that conveyed all-too-familiar emotions. It's a record both challenging and accessible, and its stripped-down DIY ethos appealed to the punk-rock crowd while the melodies drew in the older folks. Both fresh and familiar, it paid tribute to the past but simultaneously pointed the way to the future.

Costello would go on to write bigger hits, to create a more sophisticated sound with the Attractions, but there is something elemental about *My Aim Is True*, a sound that could only have been produced by a man at that stage in his life, at this stage in rock music, that he never duplicated on any other album. Like the groundbreaking roar of Jimi Hendrix's *Are You Experienced* or the fearsome sound of N.W.A.'s first outing, *Straight Outta Compton*, *My Aim Is True* captured the right sound for the right time; a perfect blend of artist, music and zeitgeist.

1

Glittering Childhood Wonder

According to Lillian MacManus, the first words to pass her son Declan's lips were "Siameses," "skin," and "Mommy." Not the random aping of sounds heard by the small child, but requests for Peggy Lee's "The Siamese Cat Song" and "I've Got You Under My Skin" by Frank Sinatra. His first vocalizations were a reflection of an upbringing surrounded by music.

Lillian, who ran the record shop in Selfridges department store ("When it was a place of glittering, childhood wonder," Elvis told *Time Out*, "and not the tacky tourist trap it seems like now"), and father Ross, a busy trumpeter and singer, welcomed Declan Patrick MacManus on August 25, 1954.

Best known for composing and singing "I'm a Secret Lemonade Drinker" for a R. White's Lemonade TV ad — listen closely and you'll hear a teenaged Declan singing backup — Ross performed constantly with the "British Glenn Miller," the Joe Loss Orchestra. During the orchestra's 14-year residency at the Hammersmith Palais and their Friday lunchtime radio show, Ross covered the big hits of the day. In 1963, the orchestra even shared the bill of the Royal Command Performance at the London Palladium with The Beatles and Marlene Dietrich, featuring her musical director, Burt Bacharach. "[Loss] would say, 'If you want to be a star, go off to a record company and be a star,'" said Ross. "'If you want to work every night and get weekly wages for as long as you want, stay with me — but don't complain.'"

To keep up with the grueling weekly schedule of learning new tunes, Ross had a special device on his Decca Decalion stereo that played a record over and over while he sang along, studying the words and the nuances of the tunes. Declan also listened — "I learned all my vocal harmony off records of that era," Costello told *People Magazine* — and often went to see his father play, especially when special guests like The Hollies sat in on the Friday radio show. "I remember how great the musicians were in Joe Loss's band, how clever the arrangements were, so simple, with just the right amount of notes."

"I knew the names of jazz musicians before I went to school," he told *The Observer*. "[Dizzy] Gillespie, Charles Mingus. I really loved Peggy Lee; and that comes from a broadmindedness that was fostered in my household from an early age."

By age 11, he (and everyone else) was a member of the Beatles Fan Club — the first record he owned was *Please Please Me* — although he wasn't a bandwagon jumper. In the years to come, he was too young to be a mod, not interested in skinhead conformity, and, as biographer Tony Clayton-Lea wrote, "too wary of the more farcical elements of glam rock," and so instead, he listened and absorbed everything.

"What a shocking thing to live in a world where there was Manfred Mann and the Supremes and Engelbert Humperdinck and here comes 'Like a Rolling Stone,'" he told *Esquire*. "That was a great world, a very exciting time." James Taylor and other singer-songwriters caught his ear for a time, but he soon tired of self-confessional lyrics. Tamla Motown and reggae were his preferred party sounds. "When I was a teenager," he told *Rolling Stone*'s David Fricke, "I didn't just listen to rock. I remember being smitten with some girl and listening to the Supremes and the Temptations doing 'I'm Gonna Make You Love Me.' But I also liked David Ackles. He didn't sound to me like a kid. He sounded grown-up — there was [also] Percy Mayfield and Kurt Weill in there."

By age 15, with all those influences swirling around in his head, he began writing his own material. In subsequent years, his restless musical spirit, fostered by his wandering ear, would manifest itself with wild career reinventions, writing and recording songs in various milieus, including country, jazz, soul, and classical.

At age 16, MacManus stepped in front of an audience for the first time, playing solo at the Crypt (also called the Lamplight Folk Club) in the basement of St. Elizabeth's Catholic Church in Richmond. "If you played an acoustic guitar," he later said, "you could basically get up there."

That debut appearance was "traumatic . . . pretty crushing." Playing a set of "sensitive teenage songs," he noticed folk superstar, composer of "Dirty Old Town," and father of the singer-songwriter Kirsty MacColl, Ewan MacColl, in the audience. During "Winter Song," MacColl's head bowed and stayed that way for the rest of the set. "I'm sure he just nodded off."

A move from London to Liverpool — home of his Beatles heroes — saw a shift toward American country–flavored rock. While his schoolmates listened to Brit rock like Deep Purple, Uriah Heep, and Black Sabbath, he spun Grateful Dead on his turntable. Years later, in *Vanity Fair*'s "Elvis Picks the 500 Greatest Albums Ever," he included four albums from this period: *Workingman's Dead*, *American Beauty*, *Europe '72*, and *Wake of the Flood*.

Discovering an affinity for the Dead's rootsy interpretation of songs like "Dire Wolf" and "Box of Rain," he snapped up discs by The Byrds, Gram Parsons, Neil Young, and Van Morrison. All country roads, however, in those days, led to The Band's *Music from Big Pink*.

"The Band were it for me," Costello told *The Face*. "I thought they were the best. I liked them because they had beards . . . It appealed to me that they looked really ugly. And they weren't boys. They were men, and all their songs seemed to be about the olden days, but they weren't dressing up as cowboys. It wasn't phoney."

With Alan Mayes (a guitar player who shared Declan's love of Crosby, Stills & Nash), David Jago, and Alan Brown, Declan began performing as Rusty, a four piece that vocalized their singer's love of roots rock. Profoundly entranced by The Band, Declan introduced influences of his new heroes into his songs. "He had all the Americanized phrasing," said Mayes. "He could sing like Robbie Robertson and Neil Young." Rusty debuted on January 21, 1972, with Declan on guitar and singing — with instinctive harmony from Mayes — on 11 songs, including Bob Dylan's "Quinn the Eskimo (Mighty Quinn)" and "I've Been Working" by Van Morrison. The night's work earned the band £7, split four ways.

Jago and Brown soon left to go to college, leaving Mayes and MacManus to carry on as a duo. They played a mix of their turntable favorites as well as new songs by Declan, like "Warm House," to mostly sparse crowds. Musicians came to see them, but Mayes reports that the only other people in the audience were "girlfriends or someone who was a friend of somebody [in the band]. There was no actual drawing power of people on the street."

A job as a computer operator at the Elizabeth Arden cosmetics firm in London gave him a chance to take all these musical influences and coalesce them into his own songs. At work, he had little to do except place tapes on giant old school IBM 360 computers and push the odd button. The monotony of the undemanding job freed up time to write songs.

"They weren't very interesting," he said to *Q Magazine* of the tunes. "It was quite funny, like anybody's first steps at doing anything, but you wouldn't want them put under the microscope ten years later. I can't even remember a lot of it. I used to play in those clubs, or the British Legion in Birkenhead, or in libraries, anywhere they'd put something on for the night. So I'd be up there with my little sensitive teenage songs, which I don't know now 'cause I can't remember any of them. But I wrote from the start, from 15 onwards."

2

A New Lowe

"Before pub rock, people used to think the ideal gig was somewhere like Guildford Civic where you could sit cross-legged and watch King Crimson pan across the stereo," said future Still Records kingpin Jake Riviera. "But with [pub rocker bands] the Ducks, the Eggs and the Brinsleys, instead of sitting there reverently impressed, you could get fuckin' legless and have a good time!"

The pub-rock revolution was a no-frills, denim-and-plaid-shirt movement bound and determined to bring a spark back into Britain's moribund music scene, or an overblown period Stiff records co-owner Dave Robinson labeled "the Stone Age of English music." As more than one commentator has pointed out, Led Zeppelin inadvertently remarked, loudly and proudly, on the moribund state of Brit rock when they named an album *The Song Remains the Same*.

"One of the things that had happened with music at that time," says writer Richard Balls, "was that a lot of groups had become distanced from their audiences. Particularly with prog rock, which was this bombastic style of music, which had increasingly been playing bigger and bigger instruments and bigger and bigger venues, but audiences physically were getting further away from the stage. You had these huge stage shows and it was all about the show of the whole thing. The dynamic between the group and the audience had become lost at that time. A lot of bands had lost contact with their audiences."

Costello keenly felt the disconnect between artist and audience. Offsetting his arty lyrics with a driving rock-and-roll rhythm, he must have been familiar with a popular saying at the time: "Fuck art. Let's dance." "People started thinking critic-wise instead of 'Can you dance to it?' or 'Is it going to make my girlfriend weak at the knees?'" said Costello to Mark Kidel of *Observer Magazine*. "They would be busy asking, 'Is it art?' forgetting that rock was never meant to be dissected, let alone included as a subject for O-level examinations, but heard on car radios and juke boxes, or bopped to at a Saturday evening disco."

"The big labels in London didn't have a clue," says author and musician Will Birch of the shift in youth culture away from the bloated excesses of '70s rock, "except for a few execs such as Andrew Lauder at UA, Nigel Grainge at Phonogram, maybe Dan Loggins at CBS, Richard Williams [and] Muff

Winwood at Island. People like Dave Dee at Warners were lovely old-school music biz types, but they were not hip to the trip. EMI, Decca, forget it. [Dr.] Feelgood had a real hard time getting a deal, and in 1974 they were the most exciting live act in the world."

"The size of some of the labels meant they had the turning circle of an oil tanker," says Richard Balls. "First of all, some of the record labels in the mid '70s weren't interested in what was happening at a grass-roots level, but even if they were interested and they had actually been aware of what was going on, they were probably too big, too unwieldy, and too up-their-own-asses at that point to do anything about it anyway."

Dozens of back-to-basics bands said screw you to the cock rock of Zeppelin, The Who, the Rolling Stones, and their ilk and turned to a stripped-down brand of music to hoist pints to. "It was a slight turning-of-the-back to the mainstream," said *A Howlin' Wind: Pub Rock and the Birth of New Wave* author John Blaney. "Led Zeppelin, prog, bubblegum bands like Sweet, Gary Glitter, all those people . . . there were quite a small clique of people who didn't like that and they were looking for something else and they happened to find it in these pubs in London."

Before pub rock, Blaney explains, the pub scene was dead. "There was something going on," he says, "but it was crap.

> That's not fair. In London, it would have been basically Irish show bands, and actually some of those Irish show bands were bloody good. They just played

the pop songs of the day. They would have looked at whatever was in the Top Ten, and they would have replicated it and done it very well. Or it was jazz. Three old blokes playing to a handful of punters who were rather disinterested — more interested in the warm beer than the hot jazz. Or maybe a bit of folk. A couple of guys with Aran sweaters doing old English folk songs. It certainly wasn't a very exciting musical scene. It was all rather dull and boring, which is why people got so excited when these bands like Kilburn and the High Roads started playing in pubs. Can you imagine walking into your local pub and Ian Dury being there? What the fuck is that? This looks interesting. It's more interesting than the two old blokes they had on last week. That's going to get people excited. It would get me excited.

Pubs had tended to be places where people just went to drink and smoke. They were havens to masculinity in a way. You could go there and have a chat with your mates, have a few pints, smoke your pipe, and do manly things that you couldn't do at home. If you were lucky, in inverted commas, there'd be someone playing a bit of jazz or a bit of folk music in the corner. Kind of dull. Something to be endured.

With pub rock, Blaney continues, the scene got livelier: "[Pub rock was] good-time music. Go out, have a few drinks, you could dance to it. When it was played in a small venue, and most of these pubs were pretty small . . . we're talking about a capacity of a hundred or so people . . . it sounded very good."

Now viewed as the cultural predecessor to punk rock, the pub-rock movement was described by future Costello producer and collaborator Nick Lowe as being "the regrouping of a bunch of middle-class ex-mods who'd been through the hippie underground scene and realized it wasn't their cup of tea." Like punk, it was a reaction to the arena rock shows — with massive stage sets, light shows, and check-out-my-big-cock guitar solos — preferring a more stripped-down, primal, accessible form of drinking music.

At the forefront were the in-yer-face Dr. Feelgood, an explosive live act *NME* journalist Charles Shaar Murray likened to "Hiroshima in a pint mug." A rough bunch of white R&B enthusiasts from Canvey Island, Essex, or "the Thames Delta" as they called it, Dr. Feelgood were a formidable force known for blistering covers of R&B standards and new songs like "Back in the Night" and the jagged "Roxette." They were crowd-pleasers, menacing and entertaining in equal measure. On stage, said singer Lee Brilleaux, "you're pushing yourself further than you should," and audiences responded.

"Dr. Feelgood is such an important band, because they influenced so many people and had that attitude," says Blaney. "They looked good and it was all stripped down. A bit like a British version of The Ramones if you like, but playing old R&B stuff. They were really important and their attitude was really important in the way they played and the way they presented themselves."

A close second in terms of pub-rock notoriety was Brinsley Schwarz, named after their guitarist Brinsley Schwarz and featuring Nick Lowe on bass and vocals, keyboardist Bob Andrews, and drummer Billy Rankin. Early on, the band lived together in a rambling old house in Beaconsfield. It was there that The Band, in the U.K. as part of a Warner Brothers tour, rehearsed, even borrowing Brinsley Schwarz's instruments. Initially their neo-psychedelic folk-rock sound borrowed from the Grateful Dead and Crosby, Stills & Nash, but after a disastrous stab at American success — a showcase at the Fillmore East in New York flopped after the plane load of British journalists they flew in arrived late, drunk, or not at all — they fluctuated between a laid-back rootsy sound and straight-ahead rock and roll. Costello was a huge fan of the band and later recorded "(What's So Funny 'Bout) Peace, Love, and Understanding," written by Nick Lowe and performed by Brinsley Schwarz on the 1974 album *The New Favourites of . . . Brinsley Schwarz.*

"Pub rock," says John Blaney, "was a way to pay your dues and that's what was important. It would give you somewhere to play and learn your stagecraft and you could do it really cheaply. It was like Lonnie Donegan and skiffle. That kind of gave birth to all those beat groups, the Beatles and the Stones and The Kinks, they were old skifflers who bought a cheap guitar in 1957 and tried to do 'Rock Island Line.' I think the pub-rock groups were the same in a way: they inspired the following generation of punks."

Mostly unsatisfied with both the glam and prog rock coming out of England, and the hippie-fied folk ballads coming out of America, young Declan drifted into the London pub-rock scene with his short-lived band Flip City. The lineup included Mich Kent (bass), Malcolm Dennis or Ian Powling (drums), Steve Hazelhurst (guitar), Dickie Faulkner (percussion), and Declan (guitar/vocals). The band's name was chosen by Costello's first wife, Mary Burgoyne, who heard the expression "flip city" sung in Cheech and Chong's backing vocals on Joni Mitchell's whimsical cover of "Twisted" from the album *Court and Spark*.

For the most part, Costello has remained mum on Flip City. Once he found fame as Elvis Costello, it was as though his past musical efforts evaporated into the ether in favor of a carefully constructed contemporary image. He dismissed Flip City's songs as "blatant imitations" and the band's gigs as "steps in my apprenticeship." What is clear from listening to demos or "pre-professional recordings" from the time (taped with Flip City at Islington's famous Hope and Anchor pub in '75 or solo in his bedroom on Cypress Avenue) is that many of the themes and tricky word use that would populate his later work were already firmly in play. "Radio Soul" (which would eventually morph into the venomous "Radio, Radio") is a love song, but to the radio, not a woman. He was also already writing anti-romantic songs, which later figured heavily in his repertoire. In "Imagination (Is a Powerful Deceiver)," he snarls, "If you wanna dance on my face, you must tell me why you lied." It's a line that wouldn't be out of place on *My Aim Is True*, and indeed the song made its way onto the *My Aim Is True* reissues in 1993 and 2001.

Around this time, Declan's solo demo earned a bit of airplay on Charlie Gillett's influential *Honky Tonk* radio show. Gillett's Sunday program had a reputation for breaking acts; he'd recently given Graham Parker and later gave Dire Straits a push. Gillett played selections from the demo, including "Lip Service" and "Wave a White Flag," for several weeks, which Costello's wife at the time, Mary, described as "one of the big moments of his life."

"They were an OK country rock band with pretentions to be The Band," says John Blaney on Flip City. "Very kind of Americana, which is a bit odd because I have always thought of Costello as being very English. I think Flip City were just another band that you would ignore if you saw them at the pub. They were doing all this American-influenced stuff, and around the same time a lot of the other bands were being a lot more English. Kilburn and the High Roads, Ian Dury writing very English lyrics. That's one of the reasons Ian Dury didn't make it in America, because nobody could understand him. I think that's why Flip City failed. They were trying to be quite American at a time when everybody — well, a lot of people — were turning their backs on that."

"Costello was the only talented person in that band," Blaney continues. "The rest of them all went off to become accountants or something. A competent bar band who you would endure. You wouldn't slam your drink down and go, 'My god, this is amazing!' You wouldn't rush out and form a record label and sign these guys up. Obviously something happened between Flip City breaking up and him recording *My Aim Is True*. He obviously found his voice."

"Flip City's young manager Ken Smith used to come to all the early Kursaal Flyers gigs in London and constantly pester us to allow Flip City to be our support act at the Marquee or wherever we were billed," said Will Birch. "We said yes, OK, but it never happened for some reason.

Costello said later that Flip City trapped him in mediocrity, but in the grand scheme of things, the band also gave him an intoxicating taste of the life of a working musician and formed the bedrock of what would become *My Aim Is True*. Several Flip City songs were reworked for the album, but the texture of the band's music, inspired by country rockers Gram Parsons and The Band, is what put distance between Costello and contemporaries like The Clash and the Sex Pistols.

"Had Flip City gotten a real foothold around 1975, '76, they would have been a springboard for Costello, but it is quite possible that it could have ruined Costello's main chance," said Will Birch. "Because however great his talent, and of course it is immense, he would have launched prematurely, and without the name, and the fanfare, and the Buddy Holly spectacles that were key to his image in 1977. Elvis was damned lucky that Flip City bombed."

3

If It Ain't Stiff

In England, 1976 is remembered, by those who sweated through it, as "the long hot summer." Other things happened too, of course. The year also saw the first commercial flight by Concorde (London to Bahrain), and the Liverpool FC won the league for a record ninth time, but the weather was top of everyone's mind from June through July when the country suffered through daily temperatures that strayed into the 90s coupled with the worst drought since 1727. "That was a scorchingly hot summer of record temperatures," says Richard Balls, "so there was almost an overall sense that the whole thing was ready to blow."

In July, in the middle of this sweaty, uncomfortable atmosphere, came a record label that was to give the old-time music business the finger.

"Politically there was a very unpopular Labour government and musically things had gone stale," says Richard Balls. "BBC4 did a very good series about 1976. They ran all of the 1976 *Top of the Pops* because it was like watching a car accident. 1976 was considered to be the absolute pits of *Top of the Pops*. It was almost like circus acts. It had to do with everything in entertainment except the music. It had nothing whatever to do with music anymore. It was dancers in feather boas and animals. It was literally a complete circus.

"You had the political dissatisfaction and the bigger bands — like the Stones, The Who — were living as tax exiles in the States. There was a kind of malaise going on, and Stiff came in to fill the vacuum."

Stiff Records. Formed by Dave Robinson and Andrew Jakeman, better known as Jake Riviera. Depending on your view, they were either music industry veterans or "two entrepreneurial scamps" as *Classic Rock* called them. Robinson had worked for Jimi Hendrix in the late 1960s and managed pub-rock combo Brinsley Schwarz in the early 1970s. Jakeman paid his dues as road manager of pub-rock act Chilli Willi and the Red Hot Peppers and as early manager for Dr. Feelgood.

With a £400 loan from Dr. Feelgood singer Lee Brilleaux, the pair set up a shoestring record company to provide an alternative to the bloated '70s music-industry machinery they thought was sucking the lifeblood out of rock and roll. "Stiff initially wanted to make records with people they loved," writer Will Birch said, citing Sean Tyla, Martin Stone, Lemmy, and Richard Hell as examples. The label's name was an ironic joke. In record company parlance, a "stiff" is a flop.

"Stiff came along at a time when people were getting a bit sick of the kind of pompousness of some of the big outfits that were doing well at the time," says author Richard Balls. "A record label that wanted to return people to grass roots music." Or as Costello saw it, "An antidote to the music that the bands trot out from their hideaways in the tropics."

"I do think Stiff came about through Jake Riviera's frustration in dealing with the major labels trying to get a deal for Nick Lowe," adds Will Birch.

The idea was simple: find new talent and make records cheaply and quickly.

"They had to do things for virtually nothing," says John Blaney. "They got all their records pressed via United Artists, so they could get 30 days credit. Most of the other small, independent companies would have to pay up front. Dave Robinson and Jake Riviera had a very good relationship with Andrew Lowder of United Artists, and they were pretty savvy to do that. That gave them an edge. They could get the records pressed, sell them all, get all the money, and then pay for it 30, 40, 50 days down the road."

They stepped into a marketplace percolating with new music, style, and ideas. In the ebb and flow of musical taste, pub rock's popularity was waning, their denim uniforms replaced by a new breed with safety-pinned clothes and an abrasive sound.

"Punk had been bubbling away for several years," says Blaney. "You could probably trace it back to '74, maybe earlier even than that. There are some articles in British magazines where they are talking about punk and tracing its roots back to the groups who followed the British Invasion. The American garage bands and up through to Queen and Bowie are punk in their definition of the word, so it had been around for a while . . . Bands like Dr. Feelgood and Eddie & the Hot Rods were exemplars of that sort of punky attitude."

"The major labels were nonplussed by punk," said Will Birch. "EMI signed the Sex Pistols, but quickly dropped them. After a brief spell with A&M, the Pistols were signed by Virgin — Branson, ever the opportunist. CBS signed The Clash but remained in total confrontation with them and manager Bernie Rhodes."

Robinson and Riviera had their ears to the ground, but Stiff was not conceived as a punk label, which made it a good fit for Costello, whose music was as undefined as the label's mandate. In a BBC radio doc on the label, Madness singer Suggs — whose run of hits on the label paid Stiff's bills for several years — says, "Most punks actually thought it was a hippie label." In actuality, it was neither a hippie label nor a punk label — even though later they released records by The Damned, The Adverts, Richard Hell, and many one-off punk singles — but something that defied pigeonholing.

"In life, things are rarely as simple as people make them out to be," says Richard Balls. "I think there has been a lot made of the prog rock versus punk, but I think the lines are much more blurred than that. Some of the people who emerged from prog rock actually ended up on Stiff. For example, Dave Stewart in the '80s had hits with Barbara Gaskin, the number-one single 'It's My Party,' which is a cover of a Lesley Gore song from the '60s, and he also had a successful cover version of 'What Becomes of the Brokenhearted,' which he recorded with Colin Blunstone from The Zombies. He'd been in bands like Egg, and Hatfield and the North, ultra prog bands."

"One of the reasons I loved Stiff, I suppose," says Balls, "is that it was a very broad church. Some of the other labels, like Chiswick, which started at roughly the same time in London, and Rough Trade started then as well and continues obviously — but if someone said Chiswick to you, you'd have a pretty good idea that it would be an edgy band . . . not a singer-songwriter, it would be a group, and the same thing with Rough Trade. It was generally indie stuff."

It was "indie stuff" that bridged the gap between pub rock and punk rock. Chiswick burst on the scene in 1975 with the release of an EP by Sex Pistols' rivals The Count Bishops and quickly established themselves as purveyors of punk and pub R&B with releases like "Keys to Your Heart" by the 101ers, the pub rock band Joe Strummer left behind to form The Clash. Chiswick launched the careers of a varied bunch, including punk protest singer Billy Bragg, Kirsty MacColl, Simple Minds (then called Johnny & the Self Abusers) and heavy metal gods Motörhead.

Rough Trade Records began life as a record shop specializing in garage rock and reggae but found its groove selling punk rock. The place became such a mecca that a bouncer had to be hired to control the crowds of skinheads who would gather on the weekends. In the DIY punk rock spirit, they took steps toward becoming a label when French punk band Métal Urbain came to the store looking for publicity for a single. They established The Cartel, a distribution system that went on to spawn the label. "In whatever form it comes, music is still music," said owner Geoff Travis of the label's eclectic group of artists, which, over the years, included everyone from The Smiths to Buzzcocks and Scritti Politti.

The boon in indie labels was an offshoot of youth culture rejecting the old ways, refusing to buy into the status quo. They weren't all punk labels, but by embracing the do-it-yourself attitude these boutique imprints gripped the spirit of the time. Even amid this burst of activity Stiff set themselves apart.

"With Stiff Records," says Balls, "they had The Damned and The Adverts but they also had [comedian and music hall singer] Max Wall. What other label was going to put a Max Wall record out in 1977? So it was a broad church."

Stiff set up office at 32 Alexander Street in the London area of Bayswater. The office was chosen for its affordability and location, but hindsight reveals a metaphor buried in there somewhere as this new upstart record label was lodged on the lower floor of Pink Floyd fogey rocker Roger Waters's house.

The building became a hub for new music. Blackhill Enterprises (home to Andrew King and Peter Jenner, former managers of Pink Floyd and organizers of the early free concerts in Hyde Park with the Stones, Blind Faith, and so on), who would soon sign Ian Dury, was on the top floor of number 32. Eventually Stiff took out space at number 28 to open a store, where, according to Richard Balls, they sold their records, posters, badges, and things. Graphic artist Barney Bubbles — who defined the look of new wave with sleeve designs for bands including The Damned, Elvis Costello, Ian Dury, and Wreckless Eric — had his art studio in the basement. It became an incubator of sorts for a new generation of artists looking for a place to grow and be heard. Ballsy and ballistic, Stiff was running as a seat-of-the-pants operation, energized by its surroundings, which writer Will Birch described as "the epicenter of hip."

"I get the impression that Alexander Street was almost kind of hippie," says Richard Balls.

> A lot of the artists, let's face it, were kicking their heels when Stiff took them on. It's not like Elvis Costello's week was banged out with lots of other appointments . . . Well, maybe in his case because he was actually working, but some of the others would just go down and sit around in Stiff, chew the fat, and someone would come in with a demo and everyone would sit down and listen to it, and someone else would come in with some designs and people would look at the design for a record cover. If you sat there long enough, someone would say, 'Hey, can you put that cup of tea down and box up these records and stick them in the back of a van?' If you hung around there long enough you'd be given something to do.
>
> It was almost like a drop-in center for the artists

who were there. Robinson did some mad things. He managed to acquire some seats from an airline, and they were in the office for a time, and people would be sitting around in these airline seats. There was a lot of people lying about on the floor, coming and going, but for all that it was a working environment. It might have been laid-back, kind of a drop-in, but Dave Robinson really got his pound of flesh out of people. It was a business.

The business was made public on August 24, 1976, with the release of Nick Lowe's single "So It Goes" b/w "Heart of the City," his solo debut following his departure from Brinsley Schwarz. Recorded for just £45 (with only drummer Steve Goulding of The Rumour as accompaniment, Lowe plays everything else), the 45 featured the messages "EARTHLINGS AWAKE" and "THREE CHORD TRICK YEH" etched into the matrix, the smooth blank vinyl that circled the label.

"You are holding the first release from Stiff Records," read the inaugural press release, "a new independent record company, dedicated to releasing limited edition collectors recordings and chart smashes. Stiff favours sound over technique and feeling over style." (A philosophy that would later ring true on *My Aim Is True*.)

Stiff's maiden voyage was a slice of snappy British Invasion guitar-pop filtered through Lowe's dark lyrical matrix. It's possibly the first (and catchiest) song about a young boy cutting off his arm. The record didn't dent the mainstream Top 40, but was popular enough that Stiff was constantly playing catch up to fulfill orders. With sales of roughly 10,000 copies, it was voted one of the five best singles of the year by the *New Musical Express*, wedged between Junior Murvin's "Police & Thieves" and "(Don't Fear) The Reaper" from Blue Öyster Cult. Perhaps sales would have been higher if Stiff had figured out distribution by this stage of their business: Stiff singles were sold mainly via mail order or by independent stores and even, occasionally, from the back of a truck.

"In the mid '70s, for the sort of bands that were doing well, the single just wasn't an important format," said Richard Balls. "It was long-playing records. And that was what a lot of the big labels were interested in, because you could actually make a lot more money from a long player than you could from a single. You get a lot more returns from an album. The big labels weren't going to put a lot of effort into singles and that's why in the '70s most of the singles that came out were in plain bags."

Forty-five revolutions per minute turned out to be an ideal way to introduce artists and break new music — and Stiff was instrumental in reintroducing the single as a potent marketing force. Metaphorically 45s were an antidote to the bloated excesses of the double album, and practically singles appealed to indie labels who saw them as cheap and effective. The Desperate Bicycles summed it up in the song "The Medium Was Tedium" — "It was easy, it was cheap!" — while the punters, hungry for new sounds, glommed on to the short, snappy, and financially accessible records.

The indies could also take risks the majors simply would never consider. With no board of directors to answer to, labels like Stiff and Rough Trade embraced the tenure of the times, releasing singles that tackled hot-button topics like anarchy, feminism, and socialism, festooned with eye-catching and outrageous picture sleeves.

From the beginning, Riviera and Robinson understood the importance of promotion. Riviera promoted Chilli Willi and the Red Hot Peppers' second album, *Bongos Over Balham*, with a special package put together for critics. In addition to the usual stickers and badges, he also included some other, more memorable materials, including a pig's trotter and a vibrator.

Eye-grabbing slogans became Stiff's trademark. "Made the way they don't make them anymore," "Where the fun never sets," "You can tell a company by the artists it keeps," and "The vinyl is final" are among the dozens of catchphrases that adorned posters, shirts, and labels. One album cover proudly bragged, "Contains no hit singles whatsoever" and Stiff dark-humoredly called themselves "undertakers to the industry." The most famous of all, "If it ain't Stiff, it ain't worth a fuck," was the perfect mix for the times — cheeky and catchy. The Stiff brand became as important as the music it promoted. Just as sports teams have fans who follow them win or lose, Stiff cultivated a rabid fan base by curating an ear-friendly and cutting-edge roster with its signature mischievous style.

Going head-to-head with the majors required some rough-and-ready tactics. Ian Dury's second album, *Do It Yourself*, was released in 1979 with 31 different covers, each one depicting a different style of Crown Wallpaper. Stiff counted on Dury's fans — and there were lots of them, given the 90-week chart run of his last album, *New Boots and Panties!!* — wanting to buy as many of the covers as they could find. And they did. To alert everyone else to the existence of the record, Stiff staffers remodeled the wallpaper at record stores, unannounced.

"It was a hive of activity," said Richard Balls. "A very creative label with brilliant designers, brilliant marketers, all that. Also, the kind of acts they had almost had to be marketed in that way."

People had come to expect above-and-beyond marketing antics as part of the Stiff brand, but the estimable weight the label brought to their point-of-sale pranks helped oddball artists like Wreckless Eric (a strange songwriter, known for shambolic performances, who went on to have a hit with the two-chord wonder "Whole Wide World") make a mark.

"Stiff was cheeky," said John Blaney. "It couldn't happen now, and if it had come along a year later, it probably wouldn't have worked. It was a perfect storm. It was the right place at the right time with the right people. Nick Lowe was sitting around doing nothing. Dave Robinson said, 'Right, get in the studio and start producing people.' The right people turned up. Wreckless Eric. No one else would have signed Wreckless Eric. Who would have thought he'd actually become a really good songwriter?"

"One of the reasons it was so interesting was that Riviera and Robinson were characters," said Richard Balls, "but ultimately they were massive music fans. The people who were there were music fans, first and foremost. They weren't just in it to turn this stuff over for profit; they loved the music and they were very, very keen on songwriters." A retrospective look at their early output bears this out. Wreckless Eric may have been enough of a pain in the ass to send other record execs running in the opposite direction, but Stiff recognized "Whole Wide World" as a great song and signed him anyway.

As word of Stiff's antics circulated, songwriters and musicians showed up at their door, demos in hand. One of those had been turned down by virtually every other label and publisher in town.

"I had this idea that I was a songwriter rather than a performer," Costello told *Rolling Stone* writer David Fricke. "I'd been to all the major publishers. I'd give them tapes with 30 songs on them, go in, and make them listen to me play, because I'd seen that in the movies: 'I've got a song for you.' I had no idea about presentation."

"For the best part of a year, I was utterly convinced that I was right and everyone else was wrong," Costello told legendary rock journalist Nick Kent. "I thought to myself, I won't get angry, I have all these songs, no one pays me any attention, but every time I heard the terrible stuff on the radio, I got the feeling that I couldn't be wrong. And that the record labels were wrong to keep rejecting me."

Reading about Stiff in *Melody Maker* and realizing it was only a couple of stops on the tube away from the "vanity factory," he called in sick and hopped the train to destiny. Arriving at 32 Alexander just two days after they officially opened, he left a 15-song demo — four songs of which, including "Mystery Dance," later turned up on *My Aim Is True* — at the front desk. "A charming girl [Suzanne Spiro] opened the door and politely received my handwritten tape box, and that was that," he wrote in the liner notes for Rhino re-release of *My Aim Is True*. "No big interview, no audition, no cigar-chomping mogul." He bought a copy of "So It Goes" before saying goodbye and exited Alexander Street, heading for the tube station.

"It all sounds like the most romantic coincidence of all," Costello remembered in Will Birch's book *No Sleep Till Canvey Island*. "But, as I was going down the stairs, Nick was coming up and I said to him, 'Here's your new record . . .' He asked me whether I was still with Flip City. I had my guitar over my shoulder, because I'd been prepared to do an audition at Stiff there and then." Nick Lowe continued the story in *Rolling Stone*: "I ran into him at the tube station and asked how he was getting on. He said, 'Not very well.'"

Lowe told *Uncut*'s Allan Jones that Elvis's story was "like something out of one of those old-fashioned films where a guy walks into a music publisher's office and says, 'Boy, have I got a song for you!' And he plays it on the piano and the publisher leaps up and says, 'It so happens that Miss Fay Fontaine is next door!' And they wheel in old Fay and she sings it gorgeously and it's a fucking great big hit and our boy's away."

He went on to explain how Elvis had made the rounds at every record company in town and instead of leaving a tape, he'd insist on auditioning live. "Of course, they were appalled," Lowe said. "There's something very intimidating about sitting with Elvis — he sings at full blast, and he's got an incredibly loud voice."

Elvis explained to Lowe that he ended up singing — or "emoting away like there's no tomorrow," as Lowe described it — to uninterested executives who even took phone calls during the performance. "The guy would be going, 'Eight? Yes. That'll be fine, darling. Lamb casserole? Wonderful!' And poor old Elvis would be there wondering what to do. Should he carry on singing? Should he stop? Should he carry on singing, but try to be a bit quieter?"

"I figured a direct form of communication would do the trick," Elvis told London *Sunday Times* reporter Mick Brown. "But it never did."

"Anyway, it turned out he'd left a tape at Stiff, and when I got to the office Jake [Riviera] was raving about 'Mystery Dance,'" Lowe continued, "because he thought [Dave] Edmunds could cover it. Then we listened to the tape again, and Jake said, 'No. Fuck it. This guy can make a record of his own. He's got tons of stuff here.'"

Riviera was impressed, but Lowe didn't get it. Perhaps he had visions of the lackluster Flip City in mind, or maybe he was being overcautious, but he didn't bite — right away. "I wasn't convinced, I must admit," he said. "The song that finally changed my mind was 'Alison.' I was stunned when I heard that. I'm absolutely mad for a weep and when I'm in the humor, I'm hopeless. And when I heard EC doing 'Alison' for the first time, I wept like a baby."

A month or so after dropping off the demo, Costello

received a call from Stiff, granting him an audience with Riviera and Robinson. Costello remembered the meeting: "I didn't go in and say, 'Look, I've got these songs and, well, with a bit of patching up and a good producer I might make a good record.' I went in and said, 'I've got some great fucking songs. Record them and release them.'" It worked. Stiff took him on, with plans to release a single of "Mystery Dance." "There was no phenomenal advance. They've bought me an amp and a tape recorder," he said at the time.

After their first meeting, Costello could be found at the office either after his day job or at the expense of it. Of the early days spent in the Stiff office at Alexander Street, Costello said in the Rhino *My Aim Is True* liner notes, "It was, to say the least, a volatile place. Filing cabinets took a terrible hammering from winklepicker shoes, and the glazier had to be called when a fraught telephone negotiation concluded with a full bottle of strong cider being hurled through the plate-glass front door."

"In my job interview, I was asked if I liked *The Shining*," remembered one former employee who asked me not to use her name, "because they were comparing it to the office experience! Ha! I had a great time, it was mad!"

The bad-boy behavior may have come naturally to the aggressive pair, but Robinson and Riviera's volatility worked in their favor, and was perhaps the shrewdest marketing move of all. They understood musicians, particularly the new breed of antiestablishment players they hoped to attract, and knew anything that reeked of corporate behavior would alienate the very people they needed to survive and thrive.

4

Jimmied Up at Pathway Studio

The sounds of a generation may be created in the street, on café stages, or in the imaginations of musicians, but they are captured in the studio.

Every musical movement has a ground zero, the absence of which would leave a gaping hole in the sound of a generation. Imagine the rock and roll landscape if the echo chambers at Gold Star Studios didn't exist. Or if 2120 South Michigan Avenue had been a doctor's office instead of Chess Records. Or if the infectious beat of Motown hadn't been recorded at Hitsville U.S.A. There might have been no Fats Domino without Cosimo's Recording Studio; no Bob Marley without Dodd's Studio One; and the Rolling Stones' most fertile period — '66 to '72 — was undoubtedly fueled by the studio they chose to record six consecutive albums, Olympic

Sound Studios. The most enduring connection between artist and studio, however, must be Elvis Presley and Sun Studios. Would Las Vegas be teeming with Elvis impersonators today if Presley hadn't stopped by 706 Union Avenue in August 1953?

A lesser known, but crucially important, studio in the early days of punk and new wave was a grotty little place called Pathway Studios, hidden down an alleyway at the back of 2 Grosvenor Avenue in Islington, London.

Financed by the royalties co-owner Mike Finesilver earned from a songwriting credit on the '60s classic "Fire" by The Crazy World of Arthur Brown, the former garage turned studio has been described as the "delivery room" of English punk. It wasn't known for its amenities. Nick Lowe called it "a very, very basic, tiny little place"; guitarist Tim Crowther described it as "a bit cold and damp with a unique sweet musty smell that clung to your clothes and equipment for days afterwards"; and musician Alex Call said it was "so small that all you had just enough space to play your instrument."

"Pathway," said Richard Balls, "was like recording in a telephone box. Pathway wasn't somewhere where you would say, 'Well, where are we going to set the microphones up? Why don't we put them down this corridor, or why don't we hang them from this gable end or something.' It was basically like someone's sitting room."

The barebones 8-track setup consisted of an eight-by-eight meter performance space, with a two-by-two control booth in the corner — "Barely able to contain two people and the 8-track mixing board," remembers Costello — and an upright piano in the corner. "It wasn't plush," says Blaney. "It was an 8-track studio and even in 1976 8-track studios were old history."

It was cramped and odiferous but the small space had an outsized effect on the burgeoning pub rock and punk rock scenes. Opened initially as a private studio, it became a popular demo studio for many up-and-coming bands. Everyone from The Damned, Madness, Elvis Costello, The Police, Squeeze, Haircut One Hundred, and John Foxx to Shakin' Stevens, Siouxsie Sioux, Thomas Dolby, Alvin Stardust, and John Cleese recorded there. Dire Straits put down the demo and single versions of "Sultans of Swing" there, and the folk singer Ewan MacColl recorded his last album in the space. "A lot of the records from that time were recorded at Pathway," said Lowe. "They took them away to fancy studios to goose them up, jimmy them up, but everyone flocked to Pathway, because it had such a brilliant sound."

"We got big warm sounding mixes, and despite the cramped conditions the mixing process seemed effortless," said Crowther.

"But it was so horrible to be in there for more than two or three hours," said Lowe in an interview with the *Vancouver Sun*'s John Mackie. "You worked really quickly to get out of there. It had it all going on, and for hardly any money." Lowe would know. He became the first Stiff house producer, working mainly out of Pathway.

"Nick Lowe did The Damned, Wreckless Eric, Dr. Feelgood," said author and musician Will Birch, "plus his own

'So It Goes' b/w 'Heart of the City' 45 at Pathway. Also, one or two tracks for Dave Edmunds' *Get It*." Plus many, many others.

"Because I'd had more experience [in the studio] than either Jake [Riviera] or Dave Robinson," Lowe told journalist Robert Leeming, "I just became the house producer, but I didn't know what I was doing at all. Those were the days when if you said you were a record producer, and you could stand up in the studio and actually pretend to be one, then you actually were one. All it took was getting lucky once and hey presto, you've got a track record and you're on your way." Do-it-yourself was a guiding principle of punk rock, and Lowe, although not a punk rocker in the truest sense, certainly embraced the hands-on approach that came to exemplify record production in this period.

During those years, his producing style primarily involved "waving my arms around and telling a few jokes," said Lowe. Author Richard Balls added, "He used to take people to the pub — because he was a big sauce merchant — get everyone pissed up and then take them back and start when they'd all had a few pints in them."

At Pathway, Lowe earned the nickname Basher for his unique recording manifesto, "Bash it down and we'll tart it up later." Years later, he explained the saying (which originated during a session for a Dr. Feelgood album) to *The A.V. Club*: "People don't really call me Basher that much anymore, but that's still my belief, not to waste too much time in the studio. I don't like being in the studio much: I like to know exactly what I'm going to do when I get there, rather than have people lounging around eating Chinese food all afternoon. I like to get in there and go to work."

That was certainly the ethos on the early Stiff records he produced, like the first punk single and first full-length punk LP — The Damned's "New Rose" and *Damned Damned Damned*, respectively. Lowe says he did little other than watch the band as they tore through their raucous, amphetamine-laced live set in the studio. The result of Lowe's minimal interference was a record that connected with audiences hearing it on their stereos almost the same way it clicked with crowds in the clubs.

"We went in and bashed it down," said Brian James of the band. He admits to an overdub or two but essentially, he says, the recording was "just like a gig."

It was into this beer-soaked scene that Declan MacManus, now using the moniker D.P. Costello, arrived, ready to record.

His deal with Stiff was the most significant step forward in his career so far, but it came with caveats. Because of a shortage of funds, Stiff had no plans to release a Costello album right away. Instead they took the baby step of first recording a single — under the watchful eye of Basher Lowe — with a band of Marin County, California, expats called Clover.

Years later, singer and harmonica player Huey Lewis (sometimes billed as Hughie Louis in those years) became internationally famous as the leader of the News, but in 1976 he was in Clover, a struggling bar band, eking out a living on the U.S. West Coast bar circuit. Two albums recorded for the Fantasy label had failed to earn them an audience in America, but they'd become popular among Brit pub rockers. At a gig at L.A.'s Palomino Club, they met Jake Riviera, Nick Lowe, and "four guys in suits — Dr. Feelgood," remembered Huey Lewis in *Classic Rock* magazine. "They'd been playing a CBS convention."

By the end of the night, Lowe and Riviera had convinced the band that they could make a go of it in Britain. The band packed up and moved, shacking up in a rock-and-roll flop-house called the Headley Grange, a rat-infested country home and former rehearsal hall for both Led Zeppelin and Bad Company, in Headley, south of London.

Soon Clover had a record deal with Phonogram, but it was apparent their brand of good-time pub rock was quickly becoming a thing of the past. Clover member Alex Call wrote in his book *867-5309 Jenny*, "One could smell rotting dino-saur flesh over the aroma of the doner kebabs roasting down the street."

Punk was blooming. You could also see Johnny Rotten on the King's Road in a tattered Pink Floyd T-shirt custom-ized with the words "I HATE." "The week we arrived, I went to see the Clash at the Roundhouse," Lewis told *Classic Rock*, "and the audience are gobbing on them and Joe Strummer is covered in spit, and I'm like, 'What is going on here?'"

Stiff Record's decision to pair Clover — save for singers Alex Call and Lewis — and not some gob-soaked punk band with Costello on the single was an inspired decision. Costello had been a fan since the early '70s — both Rusty and Flip City covered Clover songs, and Costello said he played the Clover LP *Fourty Niner* until he knew every note in the grooves — and the band was at loose ends. It didn't hurt that Clover was well versed in the music Costello loved and emulated, and they helped the young songwriter flesh out his ideas in the studio. In return, Costello dragged the band into 1977, instilling a timely sense of urgency in every note.

John Blaney said, "I spoke with Dave Robinson and his attitude was 'I'm not having musicians sitting around doing nothing. They're here to work and I'm here to find them work,' so he would always be finding work for somebody. He put The Rumour together with Graham Parker, because The Rumour were still trying to get it together and not really sure what to do, so he said, 'Get out there and bloody work.' That's what his attitude was. We've got to work these people and I think Clover were probably between engagements, they were available, so get them in the studio."

As part of the sell job to Clover, Nick Lowe sent over a demo of Costello, solo, with a note from Jake Riviera comparing him to Van Morrison. That caught guitarist John McFee's eye. He had played on Morrison's *Saint Dominic's Preview* album and was not disappointed when he played Costello's tape. "I was blown away," he told *Complicated Shadows: The Life and Music of Elvis Costello* author Graeme Thomson. "It was pretty scary to hear somebody with so much conviction and such a sense of how to use the language. Great voice. He just had a lot going for him."

At a get-to-know-you meeting with Clover at Headley Grange, Elvis pulled out his green Fender and, without plugging it in, banged through two or three songs he planned on recording. Clover bassist John Ciambotti says each song was better than the last.

At Pathway, the site of his first real recording sessions, Costello was paired with Clover's John McFee on guitar and pedal steel; Mickey Shine on drums; and Nick Lowe chiming in on bass, piano, and the odd background vocal, while Costello supplied vocals, guitar, and improvised percussion.

Costello was excited to be playing with professional musicians for the first time, "players whose records I had previously hunted down in those cut-out bins," even if he was wedged behind an acoustic baffle, sharing the cramped space with an amp and vocal mike.

The planned A-side was "Radio Sweetheart," Costello's first professional recording and the only track cut at the sessions to feature an acoustic guitar. The result was a decidedly unpunk sound and radical departure from the rest of the sessions. (Pushed to the back burner by Riviera and Robinson, who wanted a harder-edged sound, it eventually became the B-side for "Less Than Zero.")

Everyone was pleased with the results of the session. "John McFee brought back a reel-to-reel tape on one of those old Wollensak tape recorders," said Clover singer Alex Call. "He played this stuff, and I mean, I was ready to quit after hearing that — it was so astounding." In *867-5309 Jenny*, Call wrote, "This mild-mannered Clark Kent of the Jazzmaster was truly a Superman of another planet, talent-wise."

The session tapes were a revelation to Costello. Hearing the rough-hewn but professional gloss of the recording made Costello realize that most of his old songs, the ones that had aired on Charlie Gillett's radio show, "just didn't speak up enough to be heard," and he began writing in earnest. "Each time I arrived at the Stiff office, I had another bunch of tunes to present," he wrote in the notes to the 2001 Rhino/Edsel reissue of *My Aim Is True*. "I wasn't stupid. When I wrote the first album, I saw that the most direct and most aggressive songs seemed to hit home. The rhythm of the times was like that." Although he wasn't part of the punk scene — he still lived in the suburbs with his wife and child — Costello had his finger on the pulse and was calculating enough to know what would appeal to contemporary ears.

Impressed with the new songs and Costello's first shot at recording with Clover, Stiff bumped up the order of songs from two, for a single, to a full side of an LP — but just one side. The plan was to split the album down the middle, with Costello on one half, Wreckless Eric on the other.

"At one point, it was seriously suggested that I share a debut album with Wreckless Eric, supposedly in the style of the 'Chuck meets Bo' release on Chess," Elvis wrote on the Rhino/Edsel *My Aim Is True* notes.

Neither artist was taken with the idea, but Costello was proactive in his sabotage. "I just happened to visit Pathway on the day of Wreckless's first session," he said. "While Mr. Lowe took him round to the pub to build up his courage, I cut enough new demos to make nonsense of this idea."

"It became apparent that I had five times more songs than him," Costello told *Record Collector*, "and that they needed to do a full album with me. A lot of those other songs didn't get recorded until later, when we needed B-sides."

Included in that batch of tunes were barebones guitar and vocal demos of "Welcome to the Working Week," "Blue Minute," "Miracle Man," "Waiting for the End of the World," "Call On Me," "(The Angels Wanna Wear My) Red Shoes," "I Don't Want to Go Home," and "I Hear a Melody."

Riviera and Robinson made the call to invest in a long player for Costello, but were still watching their ha'pennies. Riviera's ethos, born out of financial stress as much as conviction, was "If the group know what they're doing and they're ready to make a record, it shouldn't cost very much money and it should be made quickly." They would continue to record at Pathway, which at under £10 an hour was the city's most economical recording space, and with Clover, whom Riviera had under retainer.

Costello says the album was made piecemeal in six four-hour sessions between October 1976 and January 1977 (although bassist John Ciambotti remembered it as four four-hour sessions). Costello threw himself into the process, using the experience of working with older, more seasoned musicians to up his game. "I started to phone in sick again to my day job, so I could rehearse at Headley Grange [with Clover] and then travel up to London to record." Elvis recounted the experience to Timothy White in *Musician*:

When I first knew Nick, his attitude was "Hell, it's no big deal that I'm in a group! You bang three chords together and you write songs!" Up until then, because I had no experience in recording, I always thought that the more complicated the song was, the more merit it had. To some extent, he was instrumental in making me see the benefit of simplicity — and I adopted that as a creed from there on.

As a singer, I always had an understanding with him that he would let me go so far with a vocal, but if he thought I was going past it and becoming too considered and losing the feeling, he'd stop me and use the earlier, imperfect take. He'd always allow me one or two wild takes beyond what he thought was it, in case I did something extraordinary that he wasn't expecting. He taught me a lot about craft and noncalculation, and that they needn't be in conflict.

Lowe wouldn't let them repair any mistakes — "Nobody will hear it in the morning" was his standard line — because, as Ciambotti recalled, "the feel was so amazing." Also, he added, they had to make it to the pub before closing time.

When the decision was made to record an entire Costello album, Clover's instrumental lineup — including keyboard player Sean Hopper and bassist John Ciambotti, who Costello called "the most outgoing and wickedly humored of the outfit" — was brought in, although to avoid problems with Clover's label, Phonogram, the band was jokingly redubbed The Shamrocks for the sessions.

Dividing their time between the musical hubs of Headley Grange and Pathway Studio, the band and newcomer quickly forged a bond. The songs were so new they sometimes didn't have titles, or at least not names the band could remember. As a result, a shorthand developed. "Red Shoes," for instance, became "the one that sounds like The Byrds."

Songs developed in rehearsals, led by ideas from the young songwriter. Feeling inexperienced, he says Clover's reputation meant that it "was pretty intimidating to ask for changes in the arrangements." Ciambotti remembered it differently: "I don't think being intimidated is in his nature!"

In studio, the songs were mostly captured on the first take. "Clover considered themselves the best band in the world," said Ciambotti in a newsletter published by Bob Lefsetz. "We grew up playing all the clubs in NoCal [northern California] practically every day for years. The reason we could do those Elvis tracks on first take is that our chops were fine-tuned on the road."

"The group picked up the feel of tunes like 'Sneaky Feelings,' 'Pay It Back' and 'Blame It on Cain' with ease," says Costello. "Perhaps they were not quite so sure what was going on in songs like 'Welcome to the Working Week,' 'I'm Not Angry,' and 'Waiting for the End of the World,' but they were recorded before we could worry much about it."

"When I think about how Nick produced this record, I have a mental picture of a big cloud of Senior Service smoke and his arms waving wildly about the tiny control booth," wrote Costello in the Rhino/Edsel *My Aim Is True* liner notes. "He was emotional, hilarious, incredibly enthusiastic, and generous, though I certainly wouldn't have embarrassed him by saying any of this at the time. He was just being Nick. Whatever he was doing, it worked."

What he was doing was keeping the sound stripped down and lean. That meant no meandering guitar solos. "In a time when guitar solos could still last for days," wrote Costello in the Rhino/Edsel notes, "John McFee was only given a few bars of 'Blame It on Cain' and 'I'm Not Angry' in which to step out. For 'Waiting for the End of the World,' he played a fuzz-tone pedal steel guitar, but his most memorable contribution is in the introduction and fade of 'Alison.' Other than that, Nick Lowe made sure that nothing unnecessarily fancy got on to the tape."

That simplicity — free from any prog rock pretension — separated the music from the big-label sound of Led Zeppelin and the like, which often favored bombast over basic performance but still had more finesse than contemporary punk records.

In total, they recorded 14 songs, the U.K. version of *My Aim Is True*'s track listing, plus "Stranger in the House" (later included as a bonus single with the *This Year's Model* LP and on several compilations) and "Living in Paradise" (included in *My Aim Is True* reissues). In those grooves, these unlikely collaborators not only laid down a collection of catchy, interesting songs, but they cut through the noise of pub rock, punk, and pop with well-crafted tunes that stressed the beauty of the classic three-minute rock song — simple, direct, angry, bitter, disillusioned, and heartbroken. And you can dance to them. On January 27, 1977, Costello and Lowe did the final mix of the album at Pathway in one uninterrupted (except for smoke breaks) five-hour session, adding a further £43.20 to the recording bill. In total, *My Aim Is True* cost £800, a trifling amount, thanks to the low per-hour studio cost and Riviera's deal with Clover, which saw them work for far less than the going session rate.

"I just love the sound of the album," Costello told *Melody Maker* writer Allan Jones at the time,

> because I love things that sound great on the radio. "Less Than Zero," I thought sounded great on the radio. The record isn't for people with fucking great hi-fis. I'm not interested in those people, or that kind of mentality. I don't want my records to be used to demonstrate fucking stereos in Lasky's. I just want people to listen to the fucking music.
>
> [. . .] the sound, the tone of the whole record is for the most part Nick's job. That's why he's the producer. At a big record company, they could have made me sound very different, maybe they would have wanted me to be the new Bob Dylan, the new Bruce Springsteen, or the new Graham Parker.

The big companies have a tendency to do that. They had quite possibly even less imagination than all these journalists, who also wanted to make me into the next "new somebody." Instead of just accepting me as Elvis Costello and making the best of it.

Costello was being bred as an independent brand who could stand apart from established acts.

It was a record that one writer noted sounded like a collection of Top Ten singles. Emblematic of the Stiff mandate, *My Aim Is True* championed "sound over technique and feeling over style." There was just one problem: how to sell it? Elvis had made the music, now Stiff had to create a public image for the musician.

5

New Name, New Look

In an era when it wasn't possible to gob off a stage without hitting someone named Rat Scabies, Ari Up, or Poly Styrene, a normal name wasn't going to cut it: Declan MacManus needed to be reborn, christened with a *nom de punk*. He was eager for a change. When people heard the name Declan MacManus, he said, they "expected a guy in a cable-knit sweater singing whaling songs."

"Costello wasn't a Richard Burton," said author Richard Balls. "He was a kind of geeky, nerdy guy who was working at a cosmetics firm. He had none of the attributes you would normally want [in order] to sell lots and lots of records. Maybe they decided this was the best way to market someone like this: give them a daft name."

In keeping with the Stiff clan's expertise in creating

provocative slogans that not only caught the eye, but commanded attention — "If it doesn't smell, it'll never sell," "Upstairs for thinking, downstairs for dancing" — legend has it that Riviera, an ex-adman, dreamed up a new name for MacManus over a couple of pints at a West London bar. (Ciambotti remembered it differently, with Riviera bursting into a Pathway session shouting, "Elvis! That's it! Elvis!")

Declan's father had a habit of tinkering with the family name, so another shift might not have seemed like a big deal to them. His father had dropped the first "a" in MacManus while with the Joe Loss Orchestra and once recorded a version of "The Long and Winding Road" under the name of Day Costello — Costello being his mother's maiden name.

Since 1975, Declan had used the name D.P. Costello — short for Declan Patrick — but was audacious enough to merge his adopted surname with one of the most famous people on the planet: "I thought it was just one of those mad things that would pass off, and of course it didn't." Years later, the singer commented that the name became a suit of armor, almost like a Superman suit he could put on to adopt a persona, an identity to sell to the public.

"I was amazed that [Declan] took it," said Dave Robinson. "He was keen to get going and it would seem looking back that he committed himself to the idea of it, so he accepted everything."

The new persona effectively erased years of career frustration, giving Declan a career do-over. "I thought Elvis was a better name than Jesus and almost as exclusive," Costello said, and, in another interview, he added, "Then it became a matter of honor as to whether we could carry it off." Declan's dad was comfortable with the pseudonym. "I often say to people, 'The fairies stole my little boy, Declan, and brought me this genius, Elvis, in his place.'"

Copping the King's name was a risky but brilliant and savvy ploy, given the cult of personality around Elvis Presley. Like Declan's songs, which mixed a new energy with Brill Building–style songcraft, the name was a poke to the chest of the rock establishment while simultaneously paying homage to tradition. It was outrageous and fit the feel of the times without resorting to cheap theatrics, like Sid Vicious, or vulgarity, like Joey Shithead.

Los Angeles scenester and *Melody Maker* columnist Harvey Kubernik remembered when he first heard the name. "I was a bit torn by the name because I was an Elvis freak," he said. "I had seen Elvis Presley five or six times starting in 1970, so I thought, 'Wow, that took some chutzpah to call yourself Elvis Costello.' I didn't know whether it was a new name or a marketing term or pseudo name or a stage name. It got our attention, didn't it? Yes."

Often Costello had fun with the new title. When a reporter from *Oor* in Holland asked if Elvis was his real name, he replied, "Yes, it is actually an uncommon name in England, but it's true." Follow-up question? "Were your parents fans of the other Elvis, or something?" Later in the interview, he shuts down the line of questioning with a terse, "People [will] see soon enough that I'm not just a misplaced joke; I'm not trying to fool anybody. It's just a name, you know."

Not everyone was in love with the change, though. Clover players McFee and Ciambotti, both American, thought Costello would be pilloried if they toured the U.S. under the name. And there was blowback from the U.S. press, dismayed that a homegrown hero was being disrespected by the upstart Englishman. "It's unfortunate if anyone thinks we're having a go at him in any way," Elvis told the *Trouser Press*.

Years later, Costello explained the desired effect of his name change to *Record Collector*, "It meant that people would pause a little bit longer. 'He can't be called that! He is called that!' By that time, they had noticed me more than the bloke called Joe Smith."

In the late '70s, in a fit of bravado, he even changed the name on his passport; then, deciding "it was stupid," he changed it back to MacManus.

Along with the name came a makeover. His physical image was cherry-picked from rock and roll history — thanks Buddy Holly and Bill Haley — but the way the bits and pieces were assembled was new and exciting. At the request of Dave Robinson, thick-rimmed, oversized Buddy Holly specs replaced Elvis's regular, rimless frames. The Damned's Captain Sensible says they reminded him of Brains, the aerospace engineer on Thunderbirds with thick-rimmed specs. "He didn't tell us to fuck off," Robinson remembered, so the glasses became part of the Elvis Costello costume. In the book *Complicated Shadows: The Life and Music of Elvis Costello*, it's reported that Ian Gomm saw Elvis leave the Stiff building wearing the new glasses as Jake Riviera's words, "And don't fucking take them off," hung in the air.

To complete the look, his street clothes were swapped for the soon-to-be-standard new wave uniform for men: tight-fitting suit jacket with narrow lapels, drainpipe jeans rolled up at least six inches, and a skinny tie. Like the music Elvis was making, the look was a mish-mash of eras, an exaggerated old-time rocker reinvented for a new time.

"It was purely a time and place thing," said author Dave Thompson. "Elvis came along at the right time, on the right label . . . Six months earlier, he'd have been lost like Roogalator; six months later, he'd have been swamped like Any Trouble. But one thing about Stiff was, they didn't always get their timing right, but when they did, they were spot on. And Costello played ball with them, which is a very important consideration. He wanted to make it as much as they wanted him to, so he did everything they asked."

In an interview, Elvis once compared 1977 to 1966, a year, as writer Krista Reese colorfully noted, of "heady, top-down, 60 mile per hour rock when the Beatles were at their peak and a veritable fleet of new bands careened toward the public eye."

Such was the case in 1977 when records from exciting newcomers like Buzzcocks, Television, The Damned, Ultravox, The Clash, The Stranglers, Talking Heads, and the Sex Pistols vied for record-store shelf space with everything from dino rock like Pink Floyd, Santana, Uriah Heep, and Status Quo to legends like David Bowie, The Band, and Iggy Pop to disco from Ashford & Simpson, Rufus, and Chic. Then there was krautrock from Kraftwerk, sexual odes from Leonard Cohen and Marvin Gaye, and even the last wheeze of T-Rex.

Even though Elvis had been the first act officially signed to Stiff Records, he wasn't the first to release a record. Or the second. Or even the third. He told *Record Collector* that he "ended up with the 11th release on the label. All these records came through from people like The Damned and Richard Hell, which were [punk records and] very much tied to the moment, so their timing was crucial. It was frustrating for me, because I wanted to get on with it."

It was a busy year and it was into this crowded and confused marketplace that the newly crowned Elvis unveiled his first single, which in cheeky Stiff style was presented in "Reasonable Stereo" according to the label note. Released March 25, 1977, "Less Than Zero" b/w "Radio Sweetheart" hit stores before Elvis had even played a live show under his adopted name. (That would come on May 27, 1977, at the Nashville Rooms, on London's North End Road.) While the Sex Pistols suggested that there was no future (for you!), and Richard Hell said he was part of the blank generation, Elvis reminded listeners that everything was less than zero. Except no one was listening. At least not yet.

Critics were kind — David Lee Roth once joked that "music journalists like Elvis Costello because music journalists look like Elvis Costello" — although the *NME* called it "Half Past Zero," noting that it was a great record, but a surreal tune about the National Front's 1930s vintage British fascist leader had "a snowball's chance in hell" of making a dent in the Top 20, even though lyrically it seemed to be in line with punk's nihilistic ethos.

At the time Costello dismissed the single's failure with a bit of elliptical wordplay with *NME*'s Nick Kent: "I didn't want to write a real slogan song, but something 'kind of tricky.' That's why it's very difficult for people in England to get the clue of the song, because the song does not have a clue; the clue as a matter of fact is that everything means less than zero and that it doesn't measure anything."

The following month, a different mix of "Less Than Zero" appeared on the aptly named compilation album *A Bunch of Stiffs*, alongside other flops like "Little by Little" by Magic Michael and The Takeaways' "Food."

"Alison" b/w "Welcome to the Working Week" shipped out on May 21, 1977, the same week as "God Save the Queen." The latter shot to the upper echelons of the *NME* charts and #2 on the official U.K. singles chart, making the Sex Pistols punk rock superstars. Elvis's second outing was met with great reviews, but the buying public remained "overwhelmed by indifference."

A third 7-incher, "(The Angels Wanna Wear My) Red Shoes" b/w "Mystery Dance" released on July 7, 1977, met the same fate as its predecessors. Good reviews, no sales.

"'Didn't sell' is a subjective comment," says author Dave

Thompson, who worked in a north London record shop in 1977. "No punk singles were 'selling' in terms of the chart and airplay . . . OK, *Anarchy* would have, if it hadn't been banned, and the first Stranglers single scraped in lowdown. But 'punk' singles, which those early Elvis's were considered, sold to the punk crowd — and, that said, they sold at least as well as anything else at the time, and probably a little more because Stiff already had that 'collectible' cachet."

Despite consumer apathy, Stiff launched a promotional campaign more suited to an established artist than a scrappy up-and-comer with three failed singles on his resume. Forty-fives with picture sleeves, life size in-store cut-outs of the back cover shot and giant 40 by 60 posters designed by house graphic artist Barney Bubbles were Riviera's way of making sure his newest act didn't go unnoticed.

"Stiff definitely had that attitude, 'Sod it. Let's do it,'" said author John Blaney. "There might not be any money but we can get this done cheaply and it's going to look fantastic! Forty by 60 posters. No one was doing that. Of course, they had Barney Bubbles who was probably working for peanuts to design it, and all they had to do was get it printed cheaply, but it got them loads and loads of publicity. Back in those days, there were three or four weekly music magazines in the U.K. and they were all looking for stuff to write about. So if Stiff could pull a stunt on a Tuesday, the following Wednesday it would be in the papers."

"It would have been dead easy to miss him," wrote Mark Kidel in the September 25, 1977, *Observer Magazine*, "with his suburban Buddy Holly looks, except that his face stared down from every poster-filled wall, transformed into a new rock image by the inevitable alchemy of publicity."

One unforgettable stunt saw Riviera release a maxi-poster of Costello, broken up in six sections and printed separately in three music magazines. "Our credo was that people are more intelligent than politicians or big business gives them credit for," said Riviera. "We wanted to really engage with fans and, since there were so many music papers, why not come up with a collectable series?"

The image was iconic — Elvis posed à la Buddy Holly, Fender Jazzmaster guitar slung on his shoulder — but Riviera was carefully crafting an image for Costello to suit the spirit of the times.

Punk rock was born from dissatisfaction and the promise of shit jobs with no future. Riviera simply played up the more zeitgeisty aspects of Elvis's bio (the soulless, dead-end computer job, dull suburban life) and ignored the less sellable parts (the folk duo and pub rock years) to create a man-of-the-people icon, a star for the downtrodden, ignored, and safety-pinned.

In 1977 *Observer Magazine* reported that around this time, there was an exchange between Riviera and a secretary that went like this:

> "It's someone who wants to start an Elvis fan club," she said, cupping her hand over the phone.
>
> "We don't want a fan club," came Riviera's quick reply. "We want Elvis to be ordinary."

Later Riviera (semi-seriously) threatened to break the legs of anyone who spoke publicly of Elvis's early years.

As Riviera orchestrated the publicity campaign, Elvis took a major step toward stardom — he quit his day job at Elizabeth Arden on July 5, 1977; Declan was gone and Elvis had committed to his new career — but the decision was not made lightly. He had a family to provide for, and so far being a rock star wasn't paying the bills. As much as he wanted to fully commit to Stiff and his burgeoning career, he still had to provide for his wife and child, so he demanded the record label pay him approximately what he was making at the vanity factory. Agreeing to take £100 a week against future royalties, he was now a full time musician with a new record scheduled to appear in weeks.

My Aim Is True — the name was cribbed from the chorus of "Alison" — wasn't the first choice of title. The more provocative *Little Hitler* was bandied about before sense prevailed. Later Nick Lowe used that title for a tune on his *Jesus of Cool* album, prompting Elvis to write the answer song "Two Little Hitlers" on his third album, *Armed Forces*.

Released July 22, 1977, with 12 different cover color schemes, the art by Barney Bubbles featured an eye-catching checkerboard pattern that boldly touted *Elvis Is King* and framed a tinted photo of the musician (by photog Keith Morris), pigeon-toed, knees knocking, guitar held like a weapon — an image Riviera called, "Buddy Holly on acid."

Others, like *Melody Maker*, called it the "psychotic bank clerk" or "demented high-school science teacher" look. At any rate, it was a picture of a man unconcerned with selling a traditionally sexy rock-star image.

"When we put out the reissue of *My Aim Is True*," Elvis told Spin.com's Chris Norris, "they printed some of the outtakes of the cover shots. People wanted to believe that this was some sort of very aggressive image, but if you look at the outtakes, I'm laughing in almost all the shots. There was just something inherently ludicrous about that pose to me, because it was the opposite of what I felt like. I didn't feel like a rock and roll star. I was just some guy working in an office who'd written some songs. And the fact that I had this absurd name and was posing like a rock and roller with these splayed legs — it was a satire."

Costello's original plan was to give the middle finger to a self-congratulatory industry with a simple caption on the back cover, "No thanks to anybody," but he was scooped by The Damned, who emblazoned *Damned Damned Damned* with the slogan, "Thanks to no one." Rather than be seen as a copycat, he nixed the idea.

"The people who were directly involved with the album know who they are," Elvis told Allan Jones in *Melody Maker*, "and they're not the kind of people who'd be worried about credits and name-checks." More likely is that the old-school reputations of pub rockers Clover were felt to be an anathema to the album's potential customers — punks and trendsetters. For whatever reason, credits were deemed unnecessary, but the promo machine continued to chug away.

Two inspired bits of Riviera-generated promotion earned the singer attention. The first 1,000 U.K. copies of the album came with a "Help Us Hype Elvis!" insert that offered up a freebie for a friend.

> In these John Denver days, people in Framptonland are loathe to shell out on new artists. As you've bought this record we assume that you groove to the Elvis GB sound. As you know there are only two Elvis. One is fat and famous, one is small and languishes in obscurity. Stiff Records, ever keen to meet the record buying public demands, have hatched a plot that allows you to become a potent factor in El's future. Here's how our See-Elvis-Go-Gold-Stiff-Go-Broke scheme works. You pay the postage. We send the album. And all you have to do is write no more than 25 words why you like the English Elvis and send this sheet (together with postage stamps to the value of 23p) to: Stiff Records, 32 Alexander Street, London W2. We will then send a free album to the person of your choice who you think can do the most for Elvis. This offer is limited to the UK only. We are only giving away 1000 albums (Jeesus - only 1000!) so write off today and grab a small stake in shaping El's destiny. His meal ticket, your El Dorado. This offer does not apply to Island Records executives, groupies, liggers, Elvis Costello and employees of Stiff.

Soon free copies of the album arrived in the mail, emblazoned with a Bubbles-designed sticker and a mail-out sheet pasted to the front that read, "Today is your lucky day!" Mint copies of the hype enclosure sheet now go for upwards of £300.

"I thought it was funny because it was honest," says author Dave Thompson. "Although they didn't really need us to help. The press loved him, radio and TV weren't threatened by him . . . he was everyone's favorite 'angry young man,' and he convinced a lot of people. Even those who were suspicious of his media popularity were taken in by his attitude. I remember arguing that point with someone at the time, I think it was when 'Alison' came out . . . I said, and still think, it was custom written for Radio 2; he said, 'Ah, but it has depths far below the surface sheen,' or words to that effect. Which is true, but doesn't disguise the fact that the man, at that time, was a walking hit factory."

A second stunt got more attention — and had the added benefit of landing the singer in jail and painting him a rebel. Riviera knew that Elvis would soon outgrow Stiff and needed to sign with a major label to have real career longevity. Trouble was, they had all already turned him down. Hearing that CBS would be meeting at a convention at the Park Lane Hilton, Riviera hatched a plan to go guerrilla and ambush the executives.

With a practice battery-operated amp slung over his shoulder, his trusty Jazzmaster, and a helping of attitude Elvis launched an impromptu audition outside the hotel's front door. Surrounded by a protective circle of Stiff employees — some holding signs that read "Welcome to London, Home of Stiff Records" — he loudly kicked off a mini concert with "Welcome to the Working Week." "The president of CBS was there," said Elvis. "It was a perfect opportunity to let them know that we were there too."

Elvis ripped through a furious set and was midway through "Waiting for the End of the World" when a crowd began to form that included some CBS conventioneers, holding tuck bags emblazoned with the slogan "A Big Fat Thank You From Ted Nugent," drawn outside by the ruckus.

Do you know any Neil Diamond songs?" asked one onlooker.

Industry heavyweights like Herb Cohen, Frank Zappa's manager, and Matthew King Kaufman, head of San Francisco's Beserkley Records, home of The Modern Lovers, shouted, "Get down Elvis!" and even Walter Yetnikoff, president of the entire CBS empire, came out and clapped along.

The rockin' racket also attracted the police. Three cars arrived to break up the "crowd of punk rockers" that had assembled. Writing in *Uncut*, eyewitness Allan Jones described what happened after the police told Jake to move Elvis along.

> Jake's having none of it. "These people are ENJOYING themselves, man!" he shouts. "Look at them! They're clapping. They're singing . . ."
>
> The inspector's unmoved, advances on Costello. "Move along, son," he says.
>
> Costello takes a step to his left, continues singing, lost somewhere in the murky depths of "Miracle Man."

"RIGHT!" the inspector snaps, unamused by Costello's flippancy. "You're nicked."

With a splendidly melodramatic flourish, the inspector grabs Elvis by the collar and frog-marches him to the waiting police van, Costello's feet barely touching the ground as he's hauled along. The crowd, disappointed, begins to boo the police.

Arrested for busking, he was on his way to the cells when a Stiff solicitor intervened, presumably pointing out that in order for busking to be illegal, money had to exchange hands. Since Elvis hadn't had his hat out, he was technically not breaking the law.

"I don't know what was said," reported Elvis in the *This Year's Model* (Rhino/Edsel edition) liner notes, "but suddenly I was given a cup of tea, they completed the paperwork, and I was released. It was no big deal."

Except that it was a big deal in the papers, who gleefully reported on it. And more than that, the ploy worked. Three months after the stunt, Elvis signed with Columbia Records in the United States.

"[Elvis getting arrested] made the front page of the *Melody Maker*," says writer John Blaney. "What did that cost Stiff Records? It cost them a £5 fine. You can't buy that kind of publicity. I don't know what you would have had to have done to get an artist on the front page, but it only cost them a fiver. Brilliant."

"By the late '70s, extravagant PR events were seen by the

serious papers as old-fashioned, decadent, and corrupt, part of the complacent rock biz that punk sought to abolish," said Paul Du Noyer, former magazine writer and editor for *NME*, *Q*, and *Mojo*. "But Stiff were clever: they loved cheap promotional stunts that seemed funny and subversively ironic. The label had great style in that respect: the Stiff Tour coaches, the personalities of Nick Lowe, Ian Dury, and Wreckless Eric, Dave Robinson, Kosmo Vinyl, etc., all offered a cheeky cheerfulness that was a welcome alternative both to big-label manipulation and punk dourness."

"There was an insatiable demand for music news," said Pat Long, author of *The History of the NME*. "The readership for these magazines was huge: *NME*'s peak sale was in 1963, but even in the post-punk era it was selling 200,000 copies a week — and because the readership was largely students they'd pass it on to four or five friends. So in a good week, it was being read by a million people."

"Historically the British music scene was well served by weekly newspapers — and they were indeed newspapers rather than magazines," said Du Noyer.

> The *Melody Maker* catered for professional musicians and others in the industry; the *NME* was aimed more at fans, as were *Sounds* and *Record Mirror*. Very little attention was paid to popular music in mainstream media, so for detailed information about record releases and tour dates, as well as the interviews, the gossip (and those all-important classifieds), fans were

> completely reliant on music papers. And record companies found the press a very cheap and effective way to reach their target market, both through advertising and arranging access to the stars. At their best, the music papers developed into the voices of a certain youth culture. They became the forum for a generational discussion, which most thinking musicians were glad to be part of.

Long says getting Elvis's name in the weeklies was not just important in creating his career, but essential: "The weekly press was a crucial element in building a name. A favorable review could mean the difference between selling a few hundred records and being picked up for distribution internationally. The late '70s was still the era of peak major-label profligacy, but indie labels used the music press as a cheap way of promoting new artists. The staff were always favorable to bands on small labels as opposed to the majors — that underdog thing."

"I think there was an instinctive understanding, on both sides, that the audience for certain artists was largely composed of music weekly readers," said Du Noyer. "Elvis definitely fell into that category. Punk and new wave artists really needed the music press, and the music press really needed a supply of such artists. It was a world of mutual dependency. Fortunately the papers were riding high, and the supply of great new acts was extremely healthy. By the mid '80s, all that would change: we moved to an age of pop videos and glossy magazines with a different ethos."

Perhaps the best bit of promotion for the record came that summer when the original Elvis passed away on August 16, 1977. Who knows what may have happened if Presley had lived to a grand old age, but there is no question that his death provided a boon for the English Elvis, who generated controversy and hundreds of column inches at the time for the sacrilegious *Elvis Is King* slogan that decorated his album cover. Costello noted in a *Rolling Stone* interview with David Fricke, "When Elvis Presley died [a month after the U.K. release of *My Aim Is True*], it got funny for a minute. There was concern it would be misinterpreted as a cash-in."

But the advantages were greater than the blowback. Costello was thrust into the spotlight, festooning the covers of British and American music magazines and receiving mostly rapturous reviews. He was, in his words, "an overnight success after seven years." In 12 months, Costello had gone from an unsung troubadour to vaunted songwriter with a hit album and the adoration of fans. Not bad for a year's work.

6

Songs of Revenge and Guilt

Listening to *My Aim Is True* today, turned up loud for 34 minutes of audio bliss, can be a dizzying experience . . . In 1978, however, it was positively vertigo inducing.

Played front to back, it's a marvel of songwriting and of performance; a greatest-hits album with only two bona fide hits. Sprung from the punk era, it is at once completely of its time and timeless — a blast of venom, bitterness, and aching heartbreak from a singer-songwriter who struggled to find a voice, who faced rejection, and who ultimately poured all he had into 13 songs. He sings like a man on fire, wrapping his tongue around twisty turns of phrase, emphasizing musical hooks so large they could land a Great White, and emoting like his life depended on it. Maybe it did. His musical life, anyway.

In the process, Elvis Costello unwittingly redefined the

stereotype of the mawkish singer-songwriter, shaving off any soft edges to reveal a spiky, discontented underbelly. As writer Matt LeMay noted, "Punks didn't give a fuck; Elvis was sensitive enough to not only give a fuck, but smart enough to be pissed off and disturbed by that fuck." The spiritual father of cranky singer-songwriters Peter Case, Paul Collins, and Paul Westerberg, Elvis heralded an edgy sound with sophisticated lyrics that made the sensitive smooth acoustic pop of Paul Simon and James Taylor sound as current as medieval folk tunes.

Dripping with sarcasm and bitterness, *My Aim Is True*'s lyrics never feel gratuitous, however. The anger, doubt, and self-pity appear genuine, not as posturing. *My Aim Is True* captures the raw power of Elvis's inner rage in a way that his later records haven't. Elvis's anger took on larger targets in the coming years — "Tramp the Dirt Down," for example, was dedicated to Margaret Thatcher — but on this disc, he's dissatisfied with his life and disappointed by those around him, many of whom are women.

As a result, some of the anti-romance lyrics have been labeled misogynist. It's a fair charge. There is a lot of bile woven into the lyrics, much of it directed at a second person, the "you," but there is also a great deal of dark humor that tempers the vitriol. In "(The Angels Wanna Wear My) Red Shoes," he sings about being so happy he could die, only to have the woman reply, "Drop dead," and leave with another guy. In addition to being a clever piece of wordplay, it's also a great heart-on-his-sleeve line that speaks to the vulnerability of the narrator. "Joy is fleeting" seems to be Costello's overarching message here and in most of *My Aim Is True*'s songs; feelings of personal inadequacy get in the way of happiness and true love. The joke is on him, and it has left him embittered.

The brashness of the songs, coupled with Costello's unadulterated nastiness, cynical humor, and razor-sharp social commentary, wrongly got him lumped in with the punk movement. Punk valued the filth and the fury as much as anything else, while Elvis's jittery, punky rhythms played in contrast to his well-developed songcraft. There was no need to hide songwriting weakness behind a wall of sound and high-energy performance as some of his contemporaries did. The songs were strong and presented with stark, minimalist arrangements to showcase his writing. He created something beyond retro, outside punk. The idiosyncratic mix of songs doesn't have the crash, boom, bang of punk either, but lyrically they share that frank, populist spirit of catharsis so valued by the Bromley Contingent and the spiky-haired masses.

My Aim Is True, inadvertently no doubt, looked past the trends of the moment to become a pastiche of sounds bridging the gap between the punk and rock and roll that came before and after. Punks could identify with the spirit of the record, making Elvis simpatico with the safety-pinned punters, but he was only a kindred spirit at best. In fact, the jumble of genres on the album — romantic ballads, power pop, boogie, and dub jams — placed side by side makes Costello's debut the first truly postmodern record of the era and one that helped define what the post-punk sound would become.

The issue of Elvis as punk or not was ultimately settled by the man himself in an interview with Spin.com in 2009: "Punk — what nonsense that was. Or new wave — even bigger nonsense."

Rock writer Greil Marcus points out, however, that without punk there may never have been an Elvis Costello. "One of the things punk did immediately in England, in London, was to destroy all rules and all restrictions on what rock and roll was and who could sing it, who could play it, who could appear in public pretending to be a musician," Marcus told writer Geoff Pevere in 1993. "No one as geeky as Elvis Costello would have had a chance before the Sex Pistols. He was, in a sense, just another freak."

Costello said the tunes that eventually became *My Aim Is True* were written in two weeks, all bound by feelings of "revenge and guilt." In an incredible burst of creativity, he banged out song after song, all containing his soon-to-be-trademark lyrical dexterity and astute melodic sense.

"There was at least as much imagination as experience in the words of this record," he wrote in the 2001 Rhino/Edsel *My Aim Is True* liner notes. "Whatever lyrical code or fancy was employed, the songs came straight out of my life plain enough. I hadn't necessarily developed the confidence or the cruelty to speak otherwise."

Unlike the rest of the London scenesters, many of whom were living in squats and trying out new material in front of audiences, Elvis took a different route. At this time, he was a family man, often working from home, although quietly. "I wrote 'Alison' and most of these songs late at night, singing sotto voce, so as not to wake up my wife and young son. I didn't really know what they sounded like until I got into the studio," he wrote in the 2001 liner notes.

The resulting songs reflect rock-and-roll archetypes — rockabilly, Buddy Holly — filtered through Costello's idiosyncratic point of view, and distinguish themselves with their sardonic and sarcastic examinations of relationships.

The album's opening, the alarm-clock rock of "Welcome to the Working Week," comes on like a swift kick in the crotch. A no-frills, punk-pop tune about Elvis's hatred for his nine-to-five job at Elizabeth Arden's factory, it mixes and matches jittery guitars, background vocals à la Beach Boys, and arsenic-tinged lyrics.

In the song's cold open, he sings about someone with their picture in the paper "being rhythmically admired." It takes a second for the innuendo to sink in, but once it washes over you the message is clear: clichés need not apply. Elvis may sing about masturbation — not an unpopular lyrical topic in 1977 — but he's going to do it differently than anyone else. It's the album's curtain raiser and mission statement, a promise of hostility, musicality, and wordplay to come — a clever punk song about the daily grind of a dead-end job, and the lack of soul in a world being taken over by technology.

The first of the album's several woman trouble songs, "Miracle Man" — a rewritten take on the Flip City tune "Baseball Heroes" — is an uptempo rocker that sounds like a sneering two-guitar outtake from a Johnny Thunders and the

Heartbreakers record. Lyrically it's the first time the misogyny alert sounds. Layered on top of Mickey Shine's frilly drumming and cymbal accents is an angsty diatribe written from the point of view of a luckless lover, unappreciated by a girlfriend. Dominated by a woman in black patent leather gloves, he sneers his resentment and anger one line at a time.

It's the voice of disenfranchisement; a beta male cry of dissatisfaction that announces not only personal failure but also defeat in life outside the bedroom; a man who feels inadequate, humbled personally and professionally. In an era where "No Future" was not just a rallying cry but a fact of life for many young Britons, the narrator's feeling of powerlessness rings true. Though there was no shortage of musical spokespersons, Elvis became the most articulate voice of his generation (speaking for anyone who had ever suffered from insecurity and doubt), using his shortcomings to earnestly tell universal stories that resonated, instead of just settling for the nihilistic sloganeering of many punk bands. Punk had the energy; Elvis had the depth.

"Miracle Man" also showcases Costello's penchant for lyrical flights of fancy as he paints a picture of his domineering girlfriend literally as a dominatrix in leather with a ten-inch bamboo cigarette holder.

At first listen, "No Dancing" is the album's most obvious throwback to another time, complete with "Be My Baby" drumbeats and a Beatles-style chorus. What sets it apart from Sha Na Na retro kitsch is the way Costello and company run the song's familiar sounds through the Punk-O-Nator™, infusing them with the edgy spirit of the day. As an add on, Elvis sings like a '50s balladeer — but one from the wrong side of the tracks.

Themes of sexual insecurity rear their anxious head again, but this time around Elvis is the voyeur, watching a relationship crumble. Dancing becomes a metaphor for sex — when isn't it in rock and roll? — and once again the woman is the heartless harpy who shoulders the blame for the man's shortcomings. The idea that women control men and control relationships with sex is already a recurring theme, and we're just three songs in. Elvis may be pilfering musical styles here, but it's clear that he has already developed an idiosyncratic lyrical point of view: he's a wannabe rock star singing about *not* having sex.

Costello and Lowe take full advantage of the crude Pathway setup, recreating some outsized Phil Spector–style percussion and layers of multitracked vocals, provided by Sean Hopper (who went on to provide the same service for Huey Lewis's biggest hits of the 1980s) and John Ciambotti.

Structurally Costello modulates the tune, switching keys from major to minor, the opposite of a common songwriter's trick called the Truck Driver's Gear Shift in which songs are cranked up a tone to create an emotional uplift, usually at the end. The last verse of Whitney Houston's "I Will Always Love You" is a particularly effective — or galling, depending on your point of view — example of a key change used to make the hairs on the back of your neck stand up. Of course, Costello goes the opposite way, using the downward tonal shift to add a melancholy line of attack to the latter half of the song.

Another song of dissatisfaction, "Blame It on Cain," switches the focus from a troubled personal life to anger at "the man with the tickertape" and the sense of impotence that accompanies that anger. Twangy guitar and pained vocals underscore this tale of discontentment. Its rootsy feel approaches The Band's sound, which had been an early influence on Costello. It's the first of two songs that stress directly how Elvis is "not satisfied" but the only one that, as author Larry David Smith writes in *Elvis Costello, Joni Mitchell, and the Torch Song Tradition*, "provides the escape clause for those seeking to avoid personal responsibilities."

From "government burglars" to religion and poverty, it's a lyrical ode to the thorns in the songwriter's side. Musically it's derivative of the 1950s, but lyrically it's miles ahead of the original rockers who inspired the melody.

If you imagine listening to *My Aim Is True* as taking a journey, it starts with the pedal to metal of "Welcome to the Working Week," then there's the cruise control of "No Dancing" and "Blame It on Cain," followed by "Alison" — the first stretch where you slow down to enjoy the view.

It's the album's signature song and most requested track, the one that gave the record its title, one of *Rolling Stone*'s 500 Greatest Songs of All Time, and the tune that convinced Nick Lowe of Costello's talent and set Elvis on a pedestal above his peers.

Guitarist John McFee establishes the country-tinged ballad's downcast texture with a now classic lead guitar riff. Lilting and gentle, it sets the scene for Costello's aching lyrics of love, anguish, and barely repressed fury. Costello has said little about the song, other than to acknowledge that it contains "a secret tribute" to "Ghetto Child" by The Detroit Spinners and that it is about "disappointing somebody." He also rejects the idea that lines like "somebody better put out the big light" and "my aim is true" refer to the murder of an ex-wife or girlfriend.

As for Alison's identity, Elvis told *Rolling Stone*'s David Fricke she's a "hybrid of several people. The song is about a person growing up and realizing life isn't going to be ideal: 'I know this world is killing you.' You're not going to be this innocent girl that I first knew — and it's me that's doing it." On VH1's *Storytellers*, he said it was partially inspired by a young woman he saw working in a supermarket and his depressive (and totally imagined) idea about what a sad life she was going to have. In the liner notes of 1999's collection of songs *Girls Girls Girls*, he wrote, cryptically, that by revealing anything more about the tune's origins or inspirations "much could be undone."

Costello's words are a gem of doublespeak that can be read in many ways. "Alison" is easily the most disputed of all Costello's oblique lyrics. On SongMeaning.net, commenters suggest the song is about everything from "murdering an old flame who has moved on" to dumping Alison "cos [sic] of her annoying personality" to "Cupid's bow and arrow."

What seems clear is that it's about an ex who had since

married one of the singer's "little friends"; it's his intentions with that former flame that are open to interpretation. It's not a sentimental song — Elvis is far too canny a songwriter to pen a traditional love ballad — but rather a look at love lost and the unhappy aftermath. Its subtle yet dramatic lines are loaded with feeling, and Costello hands in the prettiest vocal on the album here, yet the song's presentation and subtext blunt any accusation of simple aggression.

It's rich storytelling, complex as any literary work and clocking in at just 3 minutes and 25 seconds. Elvis cunningly weaves a story that stays tantalizingly out of reach, suggesting that no person — a lover or, in the case of Costello, a performer — can be totally knowable. "Alison," like his best lyrical creations, blurs the line between the personal and the professional, the songwriter and his songs.

The jaunty riff that fuels "Sneaky Feelings" belies the tune's dark underbelly. An upbeat song about — you guessed it — a disintegrating relationship, it sees Elvis using his best Van Morrison vocal impression to sing about love, losing love, and how love is better in your dreams because "it's safer that way."

"There are songs where the singer is being adored, like Bad Company, with lyrics like 'baby I'm such a man,'" he told the *NME*,

> and there are songs that are tricky and funny, that deal with people that end up with the worse end of the stick. Someone like John Prine can write amusing songs about someone who is not doing very well. But

because they laugh a bit at themselves, you don't get the impression that they are not feeling that bad, or that they're that deeply hurt.

The fact that they can still laugh about it makes them win in some way or another, even if they lost everything. I do think that aspect got a little bit too much attention. Because "Sneaky Feelings" isn't about something pleasant at all. So instead of writing about "the great love I have for you, darling" or "the great lust I have for you," it still remains "sneaky feelings." Do you understand? It's not normal, it's neither respectable romantic nor respectable horny; it's more kind of weak.

In the liner notes for *Girls Girls Girls*, Elvis wrote that "(The Angels Want to Wear My) Red Shoes" was "dreamed up during the kind of hallucination that you can only have" on the ten-minute inner-city ride between Runcorn Bridge and Liverpool Lime Street stations. Costello kept the song in his head for the ride, before rushing home to play it on "an ancient Spanish guitar" and fine-tune it at his mother's house in West Derby.

"I occasionally get visions in my head that I just write down," he said of the creation of that song, "and there's no experience of having worked upon them. I wrote it all in ten minutes. I go into a trance when I'm writing, and can remember very little, like, except sitting down once with the newspaper. It can just be a mass of print, or at other times a mass of one-liners that stick out as possible parts of songs."

By this point in the album, Costello's lyrical perspective is clear, but in case there was any doubt, the opening lines of this track spell it out in no uncertain terms, attacked with his usual brio, vocalizing all the pent-up frustration of a man exasperated by daily degradation — romantic and otherwise — but one who also understands that those very ignominies have made him the man he is today. He's bought the ticket, now he's taking the ride.

"Red Shoes" is the most lyrically opaque and catchiest pure pop song on the disc. Starting with a riff that wouldn't have been out of place on any of The Byrds' albums, a litany of bitterness about a failed relationship follows before wrapping with the repeated earworm refrain.

It's one of the more conventional musical arrangements on the album, but one that showed him as an adventurous lyricist. Feisty, comedic, poetic, brimming with righteous rage, and far more concise than Bruce Springsteen's ramblings, the lyrics reveal the influence of masters like Randy Newman and Ray Davies, more so than any punk rock contemporaries. Social and sexual commentary with a literary bent, "Red Shoes" stares into the abyss of disenfranchisement with some fancy wordsmithing along the way.

A television show inspired the album's next tune, a song that became a lightning rod for controversy. "'Less Than Zero' was a song I had written after seeing the despicable Oswald Mosley being interviewed on BBC television," Elvis wrote in the liner notes for the 2001 reissue of *My Aim Is True*. "The former leader of the British Union of Fascists seemed unrepentant about his poisonous actions of the 1930s. The song was more of a slandering fantasy than a reasoned argument."

In the *Girls Girls Girls* notes, he added, "I placed Mr. Oswald in this warped and lurid fantasy. No more than he was trying to do with his own past." Just three days after becoming enraged by Mosley on the telly, Costello was at Pathway, teaching Clover the tune before spewing his venom into a microphone.

Elvis continued his anti-fascist theme on subsequent albums — in "Night Rally" from *This Year's Model* and "Goon Squad" from *Armed Forces* — but to make "Less Than Zero" relevant for a North American audience in January 1978, he changed the Oswald Mosley reference when he sang the song live. The "Dallas version" twists the original lyrics with sly references to Kennedy assassin Lee Harvey Oswald and the Zapruder film.

There are thousands of rock-and-roll songs about love, lovin', makin' love, and makin' you feel so-o-o-o-o good. Rarer are tunes like "Mystery Dance," Costello's bar band boogie ode to sexual ineptness. Once again, dancing is a metaphor for sex, but as the title suggests, it's a mystery to the singer.

It's the tune that first grabbed the ear of Stiff Records and the song that showcases the Clover musicians' chops. Taking a lead from Little Richard's "Ready Teddy," the band goes full-on rockabilly, complete with amped-up rhythm and precision dead-stops. It's a full-on rave-up, with Jerry Lee Lewis–style piano and a raging, reverbed vocal.

Lyrically it looks to classic '50s rock . . . in spirit anyway. Early rock and roll disguised sexy lyrics with metaphor, sneaking raunchy references past parents. "Good golly, Miss Molly! She sure likes to ball," indeed. Costello breathes the same metaphoric air, but goes down a different path, creating a story of a virgin learning about sex. The pent-up sexual frustration finds voice in the tune's herky-jerky arrangement, clumsy adolescent fumblings of someone who's excited but doesn't "know how to do it."

"Pay It Back" dates back to Costello's pub-rock days; the tune originally appeared on a demo tape of his early band Flip City. The demo version is lyrically and structurally similar to the later rendering, but brings to the fore Costello's love of Van Morrison and blue-eyed soul that seems at odds with the song's anti-sentimental stance.

It's another song about dissatisfaction, but one couplet stands out as, perhaps, the very heart and soul of the album, if not the motivating factor behind much of the music being made at the time: "They told me everything was guaranteed / Somebody somewhere must've lied to me." Costello was 21 when he wrote "Pay It Back," with a wife and child and a dead-end job. The song plays like his cry of disillusionment and these two crucial lines are sung with real anguish.

"I'm Not Angry" is the only song on the disc that could formally be classified as new wave. The misleading title — this is easily one of the angriest songs Costello has ever recorded — crowns a track that throbs with crashing cymbals, weird whispered background vocals, the album's only guitar solo, and a snarling vocal. It's a powerful thunderstorm of indignation and hurt.

A curt lyric about catching a girlfriend two-timing is fueled by the album's fastest tempo. It's an anthem to prideful passive-aggressive behavior, the bravado of the wounded angrily denying any animosity. The reference to the girlfriend "smiling with her legs" is harsh stuff and may be the line that got him labeled a misogynist.

Elvis says the next track, which closed the U.K. issue of the album, came to him while riding on the train. "The faster tunes often came to me when riding on the Underground," he said, and the Dylanesque lyrics of "Waiting for the End of the World" are a dark apocalyptic fantasy inspired by seeing a legendary rock writer on a late night ride on the subway.

In *Apathy for the Devil: A Seventies Memoir*, Nick Kent — described as the "Judy Garland of rock journalism" by Lou Reed — writes that the song was about Costello "seeing me almost get attacked by fellow passengers on a tube ride out toward Middlesex. I'm the guy in the first verse — or at least that's what the composer told me." Legend has it Costello was surprised at how out-of-it Kent was, oblivious to the commotion he was causing on the train.

Costello imagined the song as a Velvet Underground drone, but Clover, unfamiliar with the style, transformed the tune into groove-based blues. McFee's steel-guitar underscores Costello's strange lyrics — a mix of surreal imagery (a runaway bride, groom, congregation, and priest all board this mystery train) and gritty, downtown turns of phrase.

"Waiting for the End of the World" takes the tempo down a notch or three from "I'm Not Angry" and is the most structurally ambitious song on the original album. The only tune to feature a large number of overdubs, it also intrigues with unusual chord changes and unexpected twists — a terrific, thought-provoking blast of bluesy power pop to close the Stiff's U.K. version of the album.

The March 1978 U.S. release of *My Aim Is True* included a terse, reggae-tinged tune that became a Costello classic. "Watching the Detectives" was written and recorded quickly. Clover had moved on to greener pastures by this point and were replaced for the Pathway session by musicians from Graham Parker's band The Rumour — Steve Goulding on drums and Andrew Bodnar on bass.

Costello says he wrote the song after staying up for 36 hours listening to The Clash's first eponymous album. "When I first put it on, I thought it was just terrible. Then I played it again and I liked it better. By the end, I stayed up all night listening to it on headphones, and I thought it was great. Then I wrote 'Watching the Detectives.'"

Reggae was a driving force in the punk underground. A generation of white British punks looked to Jamaican rhythms as an alternative to the overblown rock and shiny pop music that dominated the radio. "Pop reggae had been making the U.K. charts since the late '60s; harder stuff had been growing in strength through the 1970s," said writer Dave Thompson. He notes that punks loved it "because (a) it was rebel music; and (b) because Don Letts played it all the time at the Roxy, and every club that followed felt the need to do the same thing. Then Rotten and The Clash started talking about it, playing it . . ."

As outcasts, punks and reggae audiences bonded, and soon mohawked punks were ranking and skanking to the sounds of the Mighty Diamonds, Black Slate, and Dr. Alimantado. Even Bob Marley acknowledged the trend with the 1977 song "Punky Reggae Party."

The Slits gave "I Heard It Through the Grapevine" a reggae twist, while "Nice 'n' Sleazy" from The Stranglers had a wicked growling reggae bass bed, and Stiff Little Fingers mixed and mingled punk and reggae on Bob Marley's classic "Johnny Was." The Police based their career on the reggae fusion and it also spawned the 2-Tone movement that fused ska, punk rock, rocksteady, reggae, and new wave.

The Clash tune that likely caught Costello's ear was a version of Junior Murvin's "Police and Thieves," a six-minute cover on their debut. Apparently when Murvin heard the track, which was recorded spontaneously during a break in a recorded session, he said, "They have destroyed Jah work!"

The result of Costello's sleep-deprived writing session is an epic musical noir about a man's whose amorous advances are scuttled because his girlfriend is watching TV. In an interview, he mentioned the show *Starsky and Hutch* and the rebuff, "Not now, honey, I'm watching the detectives." It's a mix of fact and fantasy with Costello touchstones — infidelity, betrayal, and murder — firmly in place. Lyrically it is ripe with arresting images, but sonically it stands out from everything that came before it on the album.

Credited to the new band, "Elvis Costello & the Attractions," the tune's skeletal minor-key melody comes in hot with Goulding's over-amped syncopated drums and Bodnar's memorable bass line. Costello's cutting guitar accents and Steve Nieve's keyboard punctuations add tension, but it is Elvis's urgent, breathless vocal that elevates the tune from reggae wannabe to a knot of emotional tension that doesn't ease up until the song fades from the ear.

Costello says "Watching the Detectives" is his favorite song from the first part of his career, and it perfectly ties up the themes of love and murder running throughout the record and shows him morphing and maturing as a songwriter.

For many, *My Aim Is True* is Costello's timely and timeless acknowledged masterpiece, setting the template for all that was to come — in terms of his lyricism and restless musical spirit — and creating the Costello universe that songwriters like Ron Sexsmith, A.C. Newman, Joseph Arthur, Paul Kelly, and Ted Leo have been orbiting ever since.

7

Buy the Fucking Record

"When the record was totally done," John Ciambotti told Graeme Thomson, author of *Complicated Shadows*, "Clover went back to the States to tour. After we got back to London, Elvis was already famous. It was fast." Less than five months after Elvis quit his job at the Elizabeth Arden factory, he was a rock star. An unlikely one, but a rock star nonetheless.

The Stiff promo department worked overtime making sure Costello's face peered out from the covers of both *Sounds* and *Melody Maker*. Inside the mags, he parried with reporters, skillfully cultivating a mythology that all but guaranteed more press coverage.

An example of his anti-rock-hero stance? "I don't really think that the past, my past," he told *Toronto Sun* reporter Wilder Penfield in 1977, "is all that interesting. I don't see any point in talking about the past. I don't want to get into that. I mean, I haven't just learned the guitar in the last 10 minutes, but I'm not going to get talking about what I've done in the past. Nobody showed any interest in me then; if you weren't there, you missed it, and that's it — it's gone . . ."

Aside from profiles, advertisements such as a full-pager for "Alison" featuring a torn photo of a model's face and the slogan "Get to know Alison — Elvis Costello did" and the simple "The best record company in the country presents the best artist/e in the world" campaign grabbed the eye.

The record filled the ears of critics, who went out of their way to praise *My Aim Is True*. Writing in *Record Mirror*, on July 16, 1977, David Brown called Elvis the "workingman's new superstar" and gushed, "Mr. Costello looks for all the world like the guy who gets sand kicked in his face on the beach, the bloke who you'd push past in the butcher's queue and know he wouldn't object, the sort who wouldn't say boo to a fly, the Buddy Holly type wall fly at the dance, but put a pen in his hand or perhaps a guitar and the real Elvis will soon emerge. And this is the beginning."

Melody Maker's Allan Jones was an early booster. In a July 23 rave, he called Elvis "powerfully individual," adding, "to paraphrase Elvis Costello's 'Welcome to the Working Week,' I think it might thrill you, I know it won't kill you. Buy-buy."

Rival music oracle Roy Carr of *New Musical Express*, in a review dated the same day, also praised the album, calling it "sexual psychoanalysis set to a dozen superb juke joint anthems." He wrote, "It takes only one glance at Costello and a couple of replays to realise that even if he may not be the predictable raw material from which teen dreams are made, he possesses more understanding of the stark reality of modern love than many vacuous song-smiths who assume they have their finger on the pulse of what goes on behind closed doors."

Matt Dickson of *RAM* credited Elvis with "reviving the almost extinct art of the hit single as self-contained pop masterpiece," and *Circus*'s Ken Tucker raved, "It's been a long time since I've had a hero. I've got one now."

Stiff's launch of Costello was executed with surgical precision, and within three days of release, *My Aim Is True* had sold 11,000 copies. Later it would become the first new wave record (a genre coined to include any pop music with ties to punk, and one Elvis, who refused to be labeled, hated and credited to "idiotic, perplexed music journalists") to break into the American Top 50 chart and would become the U.S.'s biggest-selling import of the decade.

Incendiary live shows also peaked interest. Promotion, press, and radio play aside, Stiff knew the best way to break Elvis was to put him in front of as many people as possible as quickly as possible. Roadwork is odious, a seemingly never-ending litany of gigs, low-rent hotel rooms, and bad food, but in the days before MTV, the internet, and social media, it was a crucial step in establishing Elvis as a star.

A new band was assembled to accompany Costello. In July 1977, auditions had been held to bring together the band that would play with Costello on and off for the next 20 years. The

Attractions were formed when Royal Academy of Music student and organist Steve Nason (later nicknamed "Nieve" by Ian Dury after the 19-year-old innocently inquired, "What's a groupie?") and experienced bassist Bruce Thomas were hired to accompany Costello, on vocals and guitar.

Thomas remembered, "There was an ad in the music papers and, just by the wording of it and by the timing of it, I had an intuition that it was about Elvis. It said, 'Rocking pop combo wants bass player, keyboard player, drummer.' I rang up and spoke to the girl at the office, and she said, 'Who have you played with, and what are your influences?' I told her Steely Dan and Graham Parker. They were the only two decent bands around in the mid '70s anyway. There was this kind of conversation going around in the background saying, 'Get rid of him.' 'You must give the boy a chance; he sounds like he's all right.' I think they wanted something more along the lines of The Clash. The girl that answered the phone, I actually ended up marrying a year later. In that fateful phone call, I got a ten-year career and a marriage."

The lineup was completed with the addition of drummer Pete Thomas (no relation to Bruce), recruited by Jake Riviera. The drummer had played in Chilli Willi, a band Riviera managed, and went on to play on almost two dozen of Costello's records.

In 2005, They Might Be Giants' singer and rhythm guitarist John Flansburgh wrote about the legendary show at London's Nashville Rooms on Sunday, August 7, 1977

— available as part of Hip-O's 2007 deluxe edition — for the *Daily Telegraph*. In an article titled "Gig of a Lifetime," he called the show "a genuine 'star is born' moment."

Despite advertisements boasting, "This is the place where you can see U.S. Country Stars by the dozen," by 1976, the Nashville Rooms primarily played host to a who's who of punk acts. The Stranglers recorded 1976's *Dead on Arrival* (later dubbed too raw for release) on the club's stage, and the Sex Pistols burnished their reputation as brawlers in April 1976 by participating in punch-ups with audience members.

The room only held 400 people, but on that Sunday in August more than 1,000 concertgoers jammed the place to hear Elvis and his new band The Attractions run through a set of what Flansburgh called "highly evolved songs," including nine of the tunes from *My Aim Is True*, plus unreleased tracks like "Hoover Factory" and hot off the press songs like "(I Don't Want to Go to) Chelsea."

Dave Thompson, who was also in the audience that night, remarked, "Elvis's gig sounds better on the CD than it did on the night — the place was packed way beyond what it should have been, uncomfortable and hot, and wherever you stood, there'd be at least three elbows sticking into you."

"When Costello was performing," wrote Flansburgh in *The Telegraph*'s "Gig of a Lifetime" series, "he was very inside the emotion of the songs, but in between he was almost smiley. His rock veneer had not yet hardened." That would come soon enough.

The next gig was nerve wracking for Elvis, an inexperienced traveler. Booked to appear on *Top of the Pops* on August 31, 1977, the first Stiff act to be so invited, Elvis had to fly to make the taping. "I hadn't flown since 1970," he says in the *If It Ain't Stiff* documentary, "and I'd had a bad experience." Because of a plane strike, Stiff had to fly Elvis Costello and company in a private plane. "Literally it was a rubber-band job," he said. "Two engines, six seater. I thought this is definitely Buddy Holly." They made the show, lip-synching to a live version of "(The Angels Wanna Wear My) Red Shoes." The appearance earned the band nationwide attention, but didn't help the record break the top of the charts.

Less than two weeks later, they were on stage at the large, open-air Crystal Palace Garden Party, opening for Santana. It was Elvis's first time in front of such a huge audience — 20,000-plus people by press reports of the day — and it was an inauspicious debut. Fighting against bad sound — Costello's guitar and Thomas's bass were almost inaudible — Elvis's tricky lyrics were lost on the crowd, who couldn't hear what he was singing.

To compound the technical problems, they played a set of songs unfamiliar to the dino-rock band's fan base, choosing to ignore most of *My Aim Is True* in favor of newer, unreleased material like "There's No Action," "Lipstick Vogue," "(I Don't Want to Go to) Chelsea," "Lipservice," and "Radio, Radio."

Their short set was an exercise in frustration. Jake Riviera noted that the PA system was so lame it was possible to stand underneath the speaker horns and lead a conversation at normal volume, and Chris Welch of *Record Mirror* called the audience's reaction "the biggest exhibition of natural apathy I can ever recall seeing at a rock concert at home or abroad."

Elvis's performance was impassioned, perhaps fueled by his anger at the situation, but, as Welch noted, the audience didn't care. "At one point, I observed exactly two people out of an estimated crowd of 20,000 clapping," wrote Welch, "and they were both in the press enclosure."

The next big series of shows came in October when Elvis joined Nick Lowe's Last Chicken in the Shop, Wreckless Eric & the New Rockets, former Motörhead guitarist Larry Wallis's Psychedelic Rowdies, and Ian Dury and the Blockheads on the Live Stiffs Tour.

Conceived as a multi-act revue tour, à la Dick Clark's 1960s-era Caravan of Stars package shows, which featured a variety of acts in short sets, Robinson drew on experience in setting it up. "I always liked package tours," he said, "and so did the public." Robinson had put together a tour with Hendrix, the Move, and Pink Floyd on the same bill in 1968 and with Riviera did the 1975 Naughty Rhythms tour with a number of semi-obscure acts like Dr. Feelgood, Kokomo, and Chilli Willi. Naughty Rhythms was successful and produced a live album that is regarded as the definitive document of pub rock. But that was then, and this was 1977. The Stiff tour was laced with tension from the beginning.

Robinson and Riviera's partnership was by this time crumbling under the weight of debt, disorganization, and the distractions of running a small label that punched above its weight. Tour dates were booked solid; their business was anything but. Just nine days before the tour was to begin, Riviera announced that he wanted out, and that he was taking Elvis, Nick Lowe, and The Yachts with him. Label manager Paul Conroy remembered the "discussion" that ended the business. "The pavement outside the office was littered with broken glass and empty cider bottles," he told writer Will Birch, "some of which Jake had thrown through the window."

Riviera agreed to go on with the tour and allow Stiff to release the new single "Watching the Detectives" b/w live versions of "Blame It on Cain" and "Miracle Man," but after that he was going to concentrate on his new deal, working with Radar Records.

The democratic idea behind the tour was that the acts would take turns headlining. Everyone was equal, all making the same amount of money, £50 a week. The bands were an incestuous bunch, with the troupe's 18 musicians doing double duty playing for one another. Ian Dury played drums for Wreckless Eric and Nick Lowe; Larry Wallis, Dave Edmunds, Terry Williams, Pete Thomas, and Penny Tobin performed in at least two bands each night. Despite the egalitarian makeup of the touring company, ego and abilities made short work of the rotating top-slot gimmick.

During rehearsals, it soon became obvious that Wreckless Eric — who boasted, "I never play anything less than a full chord" — didn't have the material to close a show; Larry Wallis only had one Stiff single to draw from; and Nick Lowe reportedly insisted on going on early so he could make it to the pub before last orders. The obvious headliners were Elvis and the Attractions — who, according to Costello, had been "once round the club circuit and we were ready to kill" — and Ian Dury, whose act had a chaotic swagger that connected with audiences.

The two most popular acts on the bill were no fans of one another. Dury thought the tour was geared toward launching Elvis's career, while Costello believed Stiff was more interested in pushing Ian's album, *New Boots and Panties!!* Both were commanding stage presences, Costello a coiled spring, Dury a showman who had a natural rapport with the punters. For Elvis and Ian, the tour became rock-and-roll Darwinism.

On the opening night, October 3, 1977, the company — the musicians, Stiff personnel, master of ceremony and sometime-Clash-manager Kosmo Vinyl, and satirical comedian Les Prior boarded a bus for the first gig at High Wycombe Town Hall. A "coach full of lunatics," as Elvis called them.

"Jake took the idea from the Stax revue, whereby a label would package all its major stars and use the same band for the lot," Larry Wallis said in an interview with Tony Rettman. "No messing around for an half an hour changing everything around, just BAM BAM BAM, wall to wall music for the duration. Everyone used the same amps and drums. The stage setup was to accommodate any and all combination of the artists involved, and there was no set running order of artists. There were to be no 'We'll go late and miss the supporting bands' as you could arrive a half an hour late and miss Elvis Costello or Ian Dury."

Nick Lowe kicked off the show and played all originals, including "I Knew the Bride (When She Used to Rock and Roll)" and the cool obscurity "Let's Eat," which on one night of the tour inspired a wild food fight between band and audience. "I remember Elvis turning to me with a slice of ham sliding down his glasses," says Pete Thomas.

Next up, Elvis and his prickly side. In the midst of a set light on songs from *My Aim Is True*, and heavy on new material and obscure covers (everything from Richard Hell's "Love Comes in Spurts" to Bacharach and David's "I Just Don't Know What to Do with Myself" an audience member loudly insisted on hearing songs they knew. Elvis's response? "If you want to hear the old songs, buy the fucking record."

A provocative and less-than-crowd-pleasing comeback to be sure, although not as demagogic as his October 13 greeting to the crowd: "I see we've got some cunts in the audience tonight." In later shows, the angry singer was persuaded to add in more songs from the album. He even introduced songs by some of his co-stars. Several nights, he played Wreckless Eric's "(I'd Go the) Whole Wide World," but stopped short of going through with his original plan of performing with a life-sized cardboard cut-out of Wreckless.

B.P. Fallon, Dury's publicist, who chose Costello's set to do some grassroots promo for his client, compounded Elvis's rancor. He threw hundreds of "Sex & Drugs & Rock & Roll" badges — "One said 'Sex &,' the next one said 'Drugs &,' et cetera," he said — into the crowd, where they landed like "heavy confetti." The crowd went crazy, pushing and shoving to try to grab a complete set of the pins, ignoring the act onstage.

Most nights the show closed with an ensemble version of Dury's hit "Sex & Drugs & Rock & Roll" performed by the entire company (minus Lowe, who was usually hoisting pints by that point).

Opening night made clear who the stars of the show were. Dury said his band "often upstaged Costello," although *NME* writer Charles Shaar Murray said, "The live Elvis experience is about as laid-back as Godzilla on speed."

With *Sounds* and *NME* running major stories on Dury and Elvis being signed to money-spinning U.S. contracts with Columbia, both were on the cusp of big-time success and were eager to assert their superiority on stage and off, although writer Dave Thompson, who saw the tour's Lyceum show, said the tension wasn't apparent to the audience. "Don't forget by that time," he said, "we'd all bought into the idea of Stiff as a big happy family with everyone helping each other out."

Quite the opposite was true. Elvis might have been a rock star, but there was no deference to his new status. Offstage, Elvis tried to stay to himself, often going record shopping while everyone was at the pub. But his standoffishness made him the butt of at least one prank by his road-crazy colleagues, who had dubbed themselves the 24-Hour Club, the rowdy band members whose motto appeared to be, "Why sleep when you can drink?"

One night as Elvis was sleeping — or, according to Captain Sensible, passed out after drinking a bottle of Pernod — and snoring at the back of the bus, they tied his shoelaces together, filled his gaping mouth with cigarette ashes, and "put fag butts up his nose." When neither of those pranks woke him, Rat Scabies allegedly dosed Elvis's legs in Zippo fuel and lit fire to him. "That woke him up," remembered Sensible. Even as a star he was still an outsider, even among peers.

Another offstage event must have further helped to break Elvis's spirit. He and the other musicians arrived at the Loughborough University gig to find a scene that could have been lifted straight out of *Spinal Tap*. Their contractually mandated buffet, which the rider stated must be stocked with "cold cuts of meat," was actually filled with tins of cat food. Seems the typo "cold cats meat" on the original contract resulted in the mistake.

Eventually the tour's rumble in the jungle atmosphere — tension between Elvis and Ian, coupled with the friction between Riviera and Robinson — and road weariness wore down the singer. "I did go strange near the end," he admitted, but it was also a prolific period that saw him pen songs like "Sunday's Best" and "Night Rally." Consumed by the temptations of the road — Elvis said, "It quickly reached a point where the tour started to take on the manifestations of ["Sex and Drugs and Rock and Roll"]" — but shocked by the excess of it all and suffering from what he called "assisted insomnia," he snuck away to the fire escape of a Newcastle hotel for some musical therapy.

"It was getting so ugly I was compelled to write 'Pump It Up,'" he told Nick Kent in *Melody Maker* in 1979. "Well, just how much can you fuck, how many drugs can you do before you get so numb you can't really feel anything?" The song was included in the band's set the very next night at Lancaster University and five days later was recorded in one take.

The tour lost money, by some estimates as much as £11,000, an amount that might have sunk a less spunky indie. But as a pure promotional exercise, it was invaluable. It blew Ian Dury's career wide open, which paid dividends for Stiff for the next few years.

The off- and onstage shenanigans were documented by director Nick Abson for a film eventually called *If It Ain't Stiff, It Ain't Worth a F**k* and an LP culled from the shows, the raucous *Live Stiffs* (or sometimes *Live Stiffs Live*), a collection of tunes that exemplifies the pure energy of the shows. Lowe's reworking of "I Knew the Bride" almost eclipses the single's recording; Wreckless's "Reconnez Cherie" is a sloppy suggestion of what a great songwriter he would become; and Larry Wallis's "Police Car" (written while high on Mandrax, watching an episode of *Police Woman*) is a tuneful punk song. But the album belongs to Elvis and Ian. Elvis and the Attractions do a full-on assault of "Miracle Man" and cover "I Just Don't Know What to Do with Myself," a tune written by Costello's future collaborator Burt Bacharach.

Dury and his crack band chime in with "Billericay Dickie" and "Wake Up and Make Love with Me" while everyone joins in for a howling, and appropriately renamed, "Sex & Drugs

& Rock & Roll & Chaos," capturing the wild, supercharged Stiff spirit.

At the time, Elvis summarized the four weeks of touring as "a failure as far as I was concerned." In retrospect, it feels more like a period of dues-paying for the inexperienced performer. A trial by fire — 24 shows in 28 days — that saw "runt of the litter" Wreckless Eric hospitalized for overindulgence, it shaved off some of the rough edges from Elvis's stagecraft and prepared him and the Attractions for their upcoming North American tour, a string of shows that would go a long way in spreading the legend of Elvis Costello to a new and huge market.

8

Prince Charmless

If not for Costello's trip across the pond in late 1977, *My Aim Is True* might be an obscurity today, a new wave relic, traded by collectors, by a guy with a funny name and glasses. The tour, culminating in an abrasive and now legendary performance on late night television, burnished Elvis's image and helped turn the record into a classic.

Elvis Costello and the Attractions made their North American debut on Tuesday, November 15, 1977, in San Francisco, the city welcoming the British invader with open arms. KSAN, a local FM radio station, had been pumping *My Aim Is True* up for months; record stores like Rather Ripped had sold out of the disc; and Clover were from just up the road in Mill Valley, lending a local interest angle to Costello's album.

The first days of the U.S. tour were a revelation for Costello, from the king-sized beds and TVs in the hotel rooms of their Howard Johnsons, to record shopping at midnight, to seeing Iggy Pop perform. Costello was taken by Iggy's ferocity and loose-limbed performance style. "I probably would have spent the whole tour hurling myself face down on the stage if I hadn't been holding a guitar," he later said.

Before stepping onstage, Costello used the opportunity to hone his combative but entertaining style of public relations, further crafting his edgy persona. In interviews, he claimed that Elvis was his real name and barely kept a lid on his disdain for Americana. Music nerds must have been shocked when he claimed his keyboardist, Steve Nieve, had never listened to ? and the Mysterians, a well-known '60s punk band that featured organ up front in the mix.

"In one of my favorite lines, I read a critic said [that] he comes across as kind of an avenging dork," said Krista Reese, who penned the first biography of Costello, 1981's *Elvis Costello*.

"Just as in Pinter, just as in Joe Orton," she said, "there was a sense of menace, always. There was a threat, sometimes comedic somewhat, but that was part of the thrill of it. A sense of danger that wasn't there in disco. Wasn't there in the Eagles. There was a sense of injected danger that was sometimes kind of fun." His edgy attitude in interviews echoed his music: tense, unpredictable, but, above all, entertaining.

According to *Rolling Stone* journalist Greil Marcus, one of the few U.S. journos not enraptured with the British import, Elvis "ate the mike" at his show at the Old Waldorf, while "playing rhythm and attempting lead guitar." He described Costello as "serious, impersonal, and not quite all there," and noted that "he never cracked a sneer, let alone a smile." He did, however, acknowledge that the "crowd was mad for Costello," although, he wrote, "I think there was a certain amount of autohype involved."

The two sold-out shows (one at 8 p.m. and one at 11) featured a heavy mix of familiar songs — nine out of 13 tunes in the early show were from *My Aim Is True*, seven out of 14 in the late show — and new material, during which, according to Marcus, Elvis communicated "the arrogance of the next big thing and the fear of the imposter who's sure he'll be shot before he gets through the third number." In the *This Year's Model* Rhino/Edsel edition liner notes, Costello wrote, "We received a pretty good welcome in the Bay Area."

Next stop was a two-night stand at the Whisky A Go Go in Hollywood. The legendary club had once been the most important rock club in Los Angeles. By the time Elvis and the Attractions took the stage for two weekend shows on November 18 and 19, the place had essentially become a punk club with a focus on local bands. For the five dollar cover charge, you got an opening act — L.A. glam girl band Backstage Pass, featuring singer Genny Body, who performed with half her face done in glamorous make-up, the other half scrubbed clean — and Elvis's 12-song set.

Rock historian and writer Sylvie Simmons vibrantly described Elvis's arrival in Hollywood: "The yellow posters outside the Los Angeles Whisky and the yellow pins handed to the punters make him out a Buddy Holly figure who murders young ladies in showers."

"I was a bit miffed because it was a short set," said Los Angeles author Harvey Kubernik, who at the time was West Coast U.S. correspondent for *Melody Maker*. "A stopout we used to call it. But it was damn good. Even though it was an abrupt show — either an abrupt ending or not a super-long set — that kind of added to that defiant stance. I liked seeing a rock combo *sock it*, and I saw that that night."

Writing about the Friday night show in *Sounds*, Simmons said, "No introductions, no hello-good-to-be-heres, just straight into the music, starting out . . . with '(The Angels Wanna Wear My) Red Shoes.' Very good it was too, rolling along with a fine steady backbeat from the Attractions and strong vocals, surprisingly so, from a singer who seems intent on appearing a joke, if only to emphasize the fact that once he starts the music, the joke's on his detractors. Elvis Costello and his band play ripe, full rock and roll." She also noted his "quite good vocal range" on "Alison" and "only slight betrayals of punkish tendencies" as he sneered at the audience.

At the second show, however, Elvis interacted with the audience when he threw a drink in the face of a heckler. The singer remembered in the liner notes for the 2002 Rhino/Edsel reissue of *This Year's Model*, "the audience consisted of young people making spectacularly misguided attempts to emulate London and New York punk style, all Halloween makeup and bin-liner dresses and a smattering of leather-skinned industry types in pressed denim, silver jewelry, and bouffant hair."

In the review, Simmons relayed how Riviera had press "thrown out on their ears" after the San Francisco show — his mantra to journalists at the time was "I'm not interested that you're interested" — but she still decided to brave the wilds of the Whisky's offstage area.

"I went backstage to talk," she wrote in an email exchange in 2013, "and he was obnoxious, as was his manager. I seem to recall Nick Lowe was sitting back there too and looked a little sheepish and apologetic at how rude they were."

Several contemporary writers ventured that Costello's aggressive stance was a little bit of make-believe. Around this time, *Rolling Stone* writer Fred Schruers described Elvis's "ogre image" as "at least partly a pose."

The age-old showbiz-ism, "When the legend becomes fact, print the legend," may come into play here. The carefully crafted fable surrounding Costello's backstory has been printed so many times, it has become the perceived truth. Riviera, as good a marketer as rock and roll had ever seen, was protective of the legend he created because it's a better story than the truth. Costello wasn't a geek genius sprung fully formed into London's punk rock scene, but a married suburban father who had struggled in country-influenced pub bands before being given a marketable makeover. That wasn't exactly a winning origin story in 1977's anti-establishment atmosphere.

Perhaps that's why Riviera refused to speak with me (Would you be available for a quick phone interview? "NO, I would not," he replied, with emphatic capitalization) or grant me an interview with Nick Lowe for this book. One other prominent player in the story wrote, "I'm not sure that I can speak to you, but will think about it. My problem is that I might upset a few folks and I don't necessarily want to do that." In rock and roll, the man makes the myth and the myth makes the man.

Costello's past is now a mix of fact and fiction but in 1977 the past and present sat uncomfortably next to one another.

A rare interview was granted to Rodney Bingenheimer, the unofficial Mayor of the Sunset Strip. It was a natural fit. Since August 1976, his show on KROQ, *Rodney on the ROQ*, has been a champion of new music in country-rock-drenched Los Angeles. He was the first West Coast DJ to play The Ramones and Blondie, among others, and had helped to break *My Aim Is True*.

Harvey Kubernik was present during the interview.

> I asked a few questions, but it was a Rodney interview and I think it was probably before the Whisky show or maybe it was the day after the gig. [Costello] played some records and was a little bit aloof as far as influences and all of that. He stated that even though he liked a group like Love, once you start saying those kinds of things, people think you sound like these people. He was very aware how the media worked. He was a very guarded person then. He's not quite like that anymore. I mean, did he want people to know his real name was Declan MacManus? Did he really want you to know he was a third-generation musician

and his father was sort of known with the Joe Loss Orchestra? Did he really want you to know that his mother was the manager of a very big record store? Did he, or management or the record label, want anybody to know this stuff?

I never bought any of this angry young man shit. Especially once I saw him play about ten times and conducted some interviews with him and saw him socially. This guy was a record collector, man. This guy knew B-sides. This guy knew matrix numbers. This guy let me know that he saw BBC sessions with his father at seven, eight, nine, ten, and eleven. This guy knew who Dusty Springfield was. This guy knew who Cilla was. This guy knew Sandy Shaw's birthday. I didn't understand the grudge against the world. He understood photography. He understood concepts of image, photo sessions. How much of it is him, or Jake, or the label? Whatever it was, this guy wanted his music heard.

As the tour continued, the Riviera promo machine worked in overdrive. Though he limited direct press access to Elvis, he worked closely with FM radio stations, many of which broadcast the shows live.

"A plethora of Elvis Costello and the Attractions shows were broadcast on FM radio," said Kubernik, "and there was a lot of tape swapping going on. I would hesitate to use the term bootlegging, but it was cool to get a tape of an Elvis Costello show in another city. But that stuff spread and FM radio was crucial as far as building a fan base."

There have been several officially released live Elvis and the Attractions recordings — like the Nashville Rooms bonus CD on the 2007 deluxe edition of *My Aim Is True*, the *Live at Hollywood High* CD, the Warner Theatre show that was included on the deluxe edition of *This Year's Model*, and the *Live at the El Mocambo* disc — but none from the 1977 tour. Bootlegs from the shows, like Chicago's WXRT FM broadcast from the Riviera Club and the WBCN FM broadcast of the Boston Paradise Theatre show, are widely available.

Kubernik also credited the American distributor with making some savvy promotional moves. He says they were on board with youth culture and treated fanzine writers "like you were writing for *USA Today*. As far as seating in a club, an open tab for nosh, or a drink deal, or advance discs or picture sleeves. The hierarchy hadn't been established yet. The traditional media, especially *Rolling Stone*, were suspect of the new music at first. It took them a while to figure it out, or jump on the bandwagon." He also mentioned the grassroots marketing. "Columbia Records gave me a box of 25 records and said, 'Give them to your friends.' I said, 'I only know a couple people who are disc jockeys, and another couple of writers.' She said, 'No, your friends!' The word-of-mouth was working."

The hype was swirling, but for the inexperienced singer, the road must have felt like it went on forever, with more shows in Marcy, New York; Philadelphia; Boston; New Haven, Connecticut. "Every billboard or shop sign seemed like the opening line of a new song, and sometimes that proved to be the case," Elvis wrote in the *This Year's Model* liner notes. "I was filling notebooks that would provide the lyrics of our next album, *Armed Forces*."

Next up was the Big Apple for a series of showcase gigs at New York City's oldest rock club, the Bitter End. The heavyweight New York press, who had the power to make or break Elvis, was mixed in their reaction to Costello. They all seemed to agree that the songs were top of the pops, but some took issue with Elvis himself.

John Rockwell (best music critic surname ever) in the *New York Times* suggested that Costello's menacing onstage presence was "as distracting and irrelevant as Leo Sayer's mime-white face," but also said the songs "are really fine examples of late '70s rock toughness — hard and driving and fiercely unsentimental, with a variety of emotion and theme that far transcends punk basics."

A rival newspaper, the *New York Post*, was over the moon for the new performer, likening him to the other Elvis, "the kid who might just show up on the doorstep of Sun Records to cut some discs."

A press showcase at New York's Ukrainian Ballroom further showed Elvis's combative attitude when he brought Nick Lowe on to do "Heart of the City" with the curt admonition to the collected press, "And you better fucking clap."

The tour ended at the Stone Pony in Asbury Park.

"Our people always loved British music and warmed up to

Elvis by the end of his show," said Lee Mrowicki, the Stone Pony's veteran DJ and unofficial historian.

> Although the sound was familiar — not too different from the bands that played around the Jersey Shore area in the '60s, the Farfisa sound — the aggression was a little unsettling because the way to get into our audience was to be cool, and Elvis was a little standoffish.
>
> He wasn't a household name back then but they were tight, although the show was short by our standards. Elvis played a very brief show, maybe a total of 40 minutes. There was really no encore as I remember. I guess they didn't know many songs back then.
>
> Because we were open from nine p.m. to two a.m., we were used to bands playing three to five long sets, and local bands had to play all night back then with no opening acts like in the '80s. What was strange to us — as opposed to clubs in NYC — was that it ended so soon. The night was still young and people were used to staying late and drinking.

"What we didn't know," added Mrowicki, "is that this was a prep show before *SNL*."

At the time, *Saturday Night Live* was the hippest showcase for new music on network television. Producer Lorne Michaels originally invited the Sex Pistols to play, but visa problems prevented them from accepting, so the other Brit flavor of the month, Costello and the Attractions, were invited instead.

On December 17, 1977, Elvis joined the Not Ready for Prime Time Players and host Miskel Spillman for a performance that would get Elvis banned from the show for more than a decade.

In January 1969, Jimi Hendrix got himself barred from the BBC. Booked on the variety television show *Happening for Lulu*, the plan was for him to perform "Voodoo Child (Slight Return)" with his full band then duet with the "To Sir with Love" singer on "Hey Joe."

They rocked hard to "Voodoo Child" but when Lulu was announcing the second song a loud blast of feedback squealed out of Jimi's guitar, obscuring Lulu's introduction to their duet.

The band then tore into "Hey Joe," but before Lulu could join them Jimi shut it down. "We'd like to stop playing this rubbish," he said, "and dedicate a song to the Cream, regardless of what kind of group they may be in. We dedicate this to Eric Clapton, Ginger Baker, and Jack Bruce."

As the Jimi Hendrix Experience blasted through a wild version of "Sunshine of Your Love," Lulu stood to the side while musical director Stanley Dorfman tore his hair out. The stunt got Hendrix unofficially banned by BBC honchos, but bassist Noel Redding later said, "The result is one of the most widely used bits of film we ever did."

Eight years later on December 17, 1977, Costello decided to pull a Hendrix on the stage of *Saturday Night Live*. The debut American tour was over, and a spot on *SNL* was the crowning glory, a nationally televised showcase on a taste-making show.

Costello said he arrived at NBC with the plan of trotting out a couple of songs from the live set, but things quickly spiraled downwards. Elvis didn't find the show funny, or edgy "as they seemed to think it was," and to compound the generally toxic atmosphere, record company "interference certainly didn't help my mood." Columbia wanted Elvis to play "Watching the Detectives" and "Less Than Zero," songs from *My Aim Is True* that would be familiar to the audience.

At the dress rehearsal, Elvis dutifully played the songs but between the run-through and the live show, his irritation grew. "I honestly believed that the words of 'Less than Zero' would be utterly obscure to American viewers," he said. Fearing that this audience would not care about a song about ex–British Union of Fascists leader Oswald Mosley, he wanted to instead play the unreleased "Radio, Radio."

Outside of the band, no one was on board with the song choice. Columbia wanted him to play the hits, and reportedly producer Lorne Michaels didn't want Elvis to play "Radio, Radio" because of the song's anti-media bias.

Showtime.

Costello's built-up rage is apparent in the first performance. On "Watching the Detectives," he spits out the lyrics, snarling even more than usual. Ducking and lunging, he plays a game of cat and mouse with the cameraman. It's a confrontational performance — Costello was described as "borderline feral" by *A.V. Club* writer Nathan Rabin — full of menace and unpredictability, a standout on a show where edgy behavior was the norm.

Sharp-eyed viewers also noticed drummer Pete Thomas's shirt, a homemade tee with the words "Thanks Malc" emblazoned on the front as a backhanded nod to Malcolm McLaren, the Sex Pistols' manager, who couldn't deliver the band to *SNL*.

According to an interview with Costello, he and the band were bored and drunk backstage, tired of being "bullied" into playing songs from *My Aim Is True*.

For their second number, Don Pardo introduces the band and, for a moment, everything seems to go according to plan. Elvis suddenly whips around, arms flailing. "Stop! Stop!" he yells at the band, before turning to address the audience. "I'm sorry, ladies and gentlemen, there's no reason to do this song here." He looks back at the band, who appear to be a bit bewildered, and says, "'Radio, Radio,' one, two, three, four . . ." before launching into a particularly spirited version of the song he had specifically been asked *not* to play.

Unsure of the lyrics, an NBC censor dashed to the control room bellowing, "Cut him off! Cut him off!" Fortunately calmer heads prevailed. Bob Liftin, the show's veteran sound consultant, rolled the dice and left the sound on, but kept his finger on the "kill" button, ready to cut Elvis's microphone if he sang anything that contravened NBC's decency standards.

Elvis wrote in the liner notes for *My Aim Is True*'s 2002

Rhino edition, "I believed that we were just acting in the spirit of the third word of the show's title, but it was quickly apparent that the producer [Lorne Michaels] did not agree. He stood behind the camera making obscene and threatening gestures in my direction.

"When the number was over, we were chased out of the building and told that we would 'never work on American television again.' Indeed, we did not make another U.S. television appearance until 1980." It was more than a stunt, it was a true rock-and-roll moment: a young singer fed up with how corporations were controlling his career, giving a very public musical finger to the suits who tried to tell him what to do. It was a move that earned attention from music fans and respect from the music press, but the ire of one very angry television producer.

Michaels was upset because apart from the obvious disregard for his wishes, Costello's stunt put the carefully timed show off schedule. Michaels banned the singer for 12 years, not inviting him back until March 1989. Elvis returned as an elder statesman, a troubadour who had left the bluster of his heady first appearance behind, replacing it with the confidence of a musician in it for the long haul. The bile of yesteryear that had helped create his angry young man persona now mellowed and mischievous, he appeared comfortable with his place in the world Declan McManus tried so hard to break into.

The final "all is forgiven" moment came in 1999 when Michaels and Costello cooked up a tribute of sorts to the 1977 broadcast. The Beastie Boys had been booked to play

"Sabotage" for *SNL*'s 25th anniversary. Introduced by Will Ferrell as "some young men we give an A for musicianship, and probably a C for attitude," the band gets about 20 seconds into the tune before Costello takes the stage with the words, "I'm sorry, ladies and gentlemen, but there's no reason to do this song here tonight." Looking more relaxed than in his 1977 appearance, he leads the band in a blistering thrashing of "Radio, Radio."

9

Elvis Is King

Listening to certain songs brings back a blast of nostalgia and emotion for me. Every time I hear "Welcome to the Working Week," I am immediately transported to the back room of the place I grew up.

It was a huge, old creaking building that moaned when the wind off the harbor blew too hard. It had once been a vaudeville theater and later a sawmill. Legend has it that one afternoon a worker sliced off one of his fingers, running it through a buzz saw. His shocked co-worker gasped, "What did you do?"

"This," said the guy, obviously in shock, as he ran his hand through the saw again, severing another finger.

By the time I lived there, it was my father's furniture store on the lower level, a warehouse in the back where the sawmill used to be, all crowned by a giant apartment where we lived.

Growing up in a furniture store had its advantages. When Elvis Costello was on *Saturday Night Live*, I went downstairs and turned on every television in the place to NBC to create my own immersive experience.

But my main music sense-memory from those years doesn't involve a dozen TVs turned on at once, but a small den — called by everyone, appropriately enough, the "little room" — where my friends hung out and listened to records and made grandiose teenage plans.

No more than 10 by 8 feet, with fake wood paneling and shag carpet that hung on to the dank smell of teenage boy, the little room was an adolescent asylum where my parents feared to tread. I spent countless hours in there alone and with friends, a stack of records and junk food purchased with our one-dollar allowances. For us, the music wasn't a background to the conversation: it was the conversation. And *My Aim Is True* spoke to me.

To paraphrase Nick Hornby's *High Fidelity*, no girl would ever love *My Aim Is True* as much as I did, or even bother with a guy who worshipped the record as I did, but I had bonded with Elvis, even though it would take almost 30 years for me to meet him. His songs are not just a part of the soundscape of my life; they define a period of my life.

My Aim Is True spent more than its fair share of time on the turntable, and to this day when I give it a spin — or, more rightly these days, click on the icon — I can picture the walls, smell the heavy stale air of the room, and see in my mind's eye a skinny teenager playing air guitar when no one was watching.

Notes

"[Loss] would say, 'If you want to be a star . . .'" Quotation from Ross MacManus's obituary in *The Telegraph*, November 25, 2011. telegraph.co.uk/news/obituaries/culture-obituaries/music-obituaries/8919020/ross-macmanus.html.

"I remember how great the musicians were in Joe Loss's band . . ." "Return of the Native" by Steve Grant, *Time Out*, November 9, 1994.

"If you played an acoustic guitar . . ." *Complicated Shadows: The Life and Music of Elvis Costello* by Graeme Thomson.

"I'm sure he just nodded off." *Elvis Costello, Joni Mitchell, and the Torch Song Tradition* by Larry David Smith.

"He had all the Americanized phrasing . . ." *Complicated Shadows*.

"girlfriends or someone who was a friend . . ." *Complicated Shadows*.

"Before pub rock people used to think the ideal gig . . ." *Nostalgia Central*. nostalgiacentral.com/music/music-genres/pub-rock/.

"the regrouping of a bunch of middle-class ex-mods . . ." "Elvis Costello's *My Aim Is True* Turns 35" by Josiah M. Hesse, *Denver Westword*, July 20, 2012. blogs.westword.com/backbeat/2012/07/elvis_costellos_my_aim_is_true.php.

"steps in my apprenticeship." *My Aim Is True* 1993 liner notes.

"In whatever form it comes . . ." "Johnny Marr interviews Rough Trade founder Geoff Travis," *The Guardian*, September 14, 2009. theguardian.com/music/2009/sep/10/johnny-marr-rough-trade-travis.

"a bit cold and damp . . ." and "so small that all you had just enough space" Tim Crowther, Ask Meta Filter. ask.metafilter.com/94567/how-did-they-get-those-sounds.

"Barely able to contain two people . . ." *My Aim Is True* 2001 liner notes.

"A lot of the records from that time . . ." "Q and A with Nick Lowe" by John Mackie, *Vancouver Sun*, October 6, 2007. canada.com/story.html?id=9342a121-86f6-4403-8943-223081679e68.

"players whose records I had previously hunted down . . ." Obituary for John Ciambotti by Elvis Costello, March 23, 2010. elviscostello.com/news/john-ciambotti/24.

"the feel was so amazing" "Clover Member Recalls 1st Costello LP" by Fred Mills, *Blurt*, April 2009. blurtonline.com/2009/04/clover-member-recalls-1st-costello-lp/.

"the most outgoing and wickedly humored of the outfit" John Ciambotti obituary.

"I don't think being intimidated is in his nature!" *Complicated Shadows*.

"The group picked up the feel of tunes . . ." *My Aim Is True* 2001 liner notes.

"I thought it was just one of those mad things . . ." *Be Stiff: The Stiff Records Story* by Richard Balls.

"I was amazed that [Declan] took it . . ." *Complicated Shadows*.

"I thought Elvis was a better name than Jesus . . ." Cited by Associated Press, August 19, 1998. apnewsarchive.com/1998/celebrity-spotlight-birthdays/id-78c0735f6c77c296ba6b29780478ca7c.

"The fairies stole my little boy . . ." "Ross MacManus: Singer, trumpeter and father of Elvis Costello" by Spencer Leigh, *Independent*, December 1, 2011. independent.co.uk/news/obituaries/ross-macmanus-singer-trumpeter-and-father-of-elvis-costello-6270103.html.

"He didn't tell us to fuck off" *Complicated Shadows*.

"Our credo was that people are more intelligent . . ." "When Music Advertising's Aim Was True," BarneyBubbles.com, November 23, 2009. barneybubbles.com/blog/archives/2797.

"The president of CBS was there . . ." *OOR* interview with Costello by Archie Barneveld and Martijn Stoffer, October 5, 1977. Translated on elviscostello.info.

"When I first put it on . . ." "Watching the Detectives (Elvis Costello & The Attractions)" by Jon Kutner. jonkutner.com/watching-the-detectives/.

“I always liked package tours . . .” “Stiff Records: If It Ain’t Stiff, It Ain’t Worth a Debt” by Pierre Perrone, *Independent*, September 15, 2006. independent.co.uk/arts-entertainment/music/features/stiff-records-if-it-aint-stiff-it-aint-worth-a-debt-415988.html.

“I never play anything less than a full chord”; “once round the club circuit . . .”; and “One said ‘Sex &’, the next one said ‘Drugs &’ . . .” “Hit Me!” by Will Birch, *Mojo*, October 1997.

“I probably would have spent the whole tour . . .”; “interference certainly didn’t help my mood”; “I honestly believed that the words . . .”; and “When the number was over . . .” *This Year’s Model* 2002 liner notes.

Selected Sources

Balls, Richard. *Be Stiff: The Stiff Records Story*. London: Soundcheck Books, 2014.

Balls, Richard. *Sex & Drugs & Rock 'N' Roll: The Life of Ian Dury*. London: Omnibus Press, 2000.

Birch, Will. *Ian Dury: The Definitive Biography*. London: Pan MacMillan, 2011.

Call, Alex. *867-5309 Jenny: The Song That Saved Me*. New York: Charles River Press, 2011.

Clayton-Lee, Tony. *Elvis Costello: A Biography*. London: Abdre Deutsch, 1998.

ElvisCostello.com.

Fricke, David. "Elvis Costello: The Rolling Stone Interview," *Rolling Stone*, September 22, 2004.

Gouldstone, David. *Elvis Costello: Man Out of Time*. London: Sidgwick & Jackson, 1989.

Reese, Krista. *Elvis Costello*. London and New York: Proteus Publishing, 1981.

Rettman, Tony. "The King of Oblivion Slings Mud," *Perfect Sound Forever*. furious.com/perfect/larrywallis.html.

Smith, Larry David. *Elvis Costello, Joni Mitchell, and the Torch Song Tradition*. Santa Barbara: Praeger, 2004.

Thomson, Graeme. *Complicated Shadows: The Life and Music of Elvis Costello*. Edinburgh: Canongate Books, 2004.

Wooldridge, Max. *Never Mind the Bollards*. London: Footprint Handprints, 2010.

Acknowledgments

I could have taken Costello's example and left the thank you and credits section blank but it took a village to make this book happen and I want to show gratitude to everyone who helped make it happen.

First I'd like to thank anyone who read all the way through the book to get to the acknowledgments. Without you there'd be no reason to put the words in the right order.

Then a giant shout-out goes to the folks at ECW: Crissy Calhoun, David Caron, Erin Creasey, Jack David, Sarah Dunn, Jenna Illies, and Jennifer Knoch. It's been ten years and four books, and I hope we get to do this dance again soon.

Thanks to the Ontario Arts Council for their support through the Writers' Reserve program.

Next, fist bumps to Bob Andrews, Richard Balls, Will Birch, John Blaney, Paul Du Noyer, John Foyle, David Fine, Harvey Kubernik, Pat Long, Ron Mann, David Marsden, Lee Mrowicki, Paul Myers, Wilder Penfield, Krista Reese, Sylvie Simmons, and Dave Thompson for taking the time to speak to me about Elvis, and to those who declined to talk to me, Jake Riviera, Tony Parsons, and Nick Lowe, among others, for making me rethink the approach to the book.

My brother Gary opened my ears to music other than the stuff I was hearing on the radio, so high fives to him for buying *My Aim Is True* and saving me from a life of Pablo Cruise. Thanks to the PMC, Andrea, for nodding and pretending to care as I spent endless nights ruminating on obscure '70s rock and to everyone else who was on the other end of my verbal ramblings.

The time I spent writing this book was filled with difficulties unrelated to the project. My thanks to Dr. Peter Stotland, Dr. Yoo-Joung Ko, and all the support staff and nurses at Sunnybrook's Odette Cancer Centre and North York General Hospital. Everything is A-OK now and I owe them my life.

Cheers to Ed Crouse; my *Canada AM* family — Beverly Thomson, Marci Ien, Jeff Hutcheson, Lis Travers, Karning Hum, et al.; my compadres at NewsTalk 1010 — John Moore, Robert Turner, Becky Coles, Jessie Lorraine, and Mike Bendixon; and the folks at *Metro* — Liz Brown and Dean Lisk — who have kept me on the front page for years now. Also to Ron Bodnar and Angela Bodnar, you make good daughters.

Finally, thanks Elvis, you make my ears happy.

Richard Crouse is the regular film critic for CTV's Canada AM, CTV's 24-hour News Channel, and CP24. His syndicated Saturday afternoon radio show, *Entertainment Extra*, originates on NewsTalk 1010. He is also the author of six books on pop culture history including *Raising Hell: Ken Russell and the Unmaking of The Devils* and *The 100 Best Movies You've Never Seen*, and writes two weekly columns for *Metro* newspaper. He lives in Toronto, Ontario.